# *Fishing*
# MINNESOTA

# *Fishing* MINNESOTA

### Angling with the Experts in the Land of 10,000 Lakes

**Greg Breining**

University of Minnesota Press

Minneapolis

London

Illustrations by Patricia Bickner Linder
Photography by Greg Breining

Copyright 1993 by Greg Breining

Originally published by NorthWord Press, Inc., 1993

First University of Minnesota Press edition, 2003

All rights reserved. No part of this publication may be reproduced, stored in a retrieval system, or transmitted, in any form or by any means, electronic, mechanical, photocopying, recording, or otherwise, without the prior written permission of the publisher.

Published by the University of Minnesota Press
111 Third Avenue South, Suite 290
Minneapolis, MN 55401-2520
http://www.upress.umn.edu

ISBN 0-8166-4176-5

A Cataloging-in-Publication record for this book is available from the Library of Congress.

Printed in the United States of America on acid-free paper

The University of Minnesota is an equal-opportunity educator and employer.

12 11 10 09 08 07 06 05 04 03      10 9 8 7 6 5 4 3 2 1

# Contents

# Introduction

## A DAY ON THE WATER

Have you ever wished you could spend a day on the water with one of the fishermen you watch on TV? Or the "pro" who wins all the fishing tournaments? Or a guide who always manages to get his clients into fish? Or perhaps the old man you watched on a stream one evening who could sidearm an ant pattern under the overhanging grass from 60 feet away to fool the big brown trout you never could catch?

I've wished that. I've wished just to go along, because "how-to" fishing advice leaves me cold. I want someone to show me.

So I asked some of Minnesota's best anglers—tournament fishermen, accomplished guides, fisheries biologists, and experienced fishermen—to take me fishing and show me how they catch fish. They did, and that's part of the story I'll tell.

But they showed me something more. They showed me that fishing is:

The silvery strike of a pike as it snatches a big jerkbait from your rod tip.

The deliberate slurp of a brown trout taking mayflies on an emerald stream that burbles in the deep shadows of a hardwood forest.

The awesome run of a steelhead racing downriver faster than anything I've known that lives in fresh water.

The unnerving appearance of a muskie, shadowing a bucktail but never striking.

The intoxicating beauty of evening as shadows penetrate the deepest reaches of a limestone canyon, where smallmouth bass rise to deer-hair bugs cast on quiet pools.

The experts showed me that Minnesota has a greater variety of fish and fishing than most anglers will ever realize.

They also showed me that fishing is this:

- ⚬ Pulling onto a spot of deep-water structure without the aid of electronic navigation equipment, relying only on landmarks and Joe Fellegy's dead reckoning.

- ⚬ Standing in a stream with Jay Bunke, taking turns casting to a stubborn brown that just won't take.

- ⚬ Crossing a treacherous North Shore stream with Shawn Perich, our hands braced on each other's shoulders so we aren't upended and swept downstream.

- ⚬ Listening to Henry Drewes get so worked up about his beloved catfish that he sees neither the flashing red light nor the state trooper at the next intersection.

- ⚬ Drinking whiskey and listening to John Herrick try to blow a Muddy Waters blues tune on the harp after a cold September rain shuts down the smallmouth fishing.

Years of experience have taught me that if fishing were just a matter of catching fish—even big fish—it would be a dull and soulless exercise. But add drama, beauty, humor, mystery, challenge, and personality—then fishing becomes a thing of wonder, a ritual that leads to a deeper understanding of our natural world and celebrates the very impulses that make us human.

# Chapter One

## NORTH SHORE STEELHEAD:
### *More Like Hunting than Fishing*

Every spring, as runoff surges down the steep river canyons of Lake Superior's North Shore, dozens of water witches appear at the mouths of the Lester, Sucker, Baptism, Poplar, Devil Track, Brule, and other streams large and small, working their magic with dowsing rods that remarkably resemble graphite fly rods. They hold these wands above the impenetrable, rushing water and concentrate as intently as if they were Moses, beseeching God to part the Red Sea.

Then someone calls out, "Fish on!" A torpedo of lustrous silver, rose, and olive rockets from the dark water. And a fish that has spent the most determined moments of its life ascending a raging stream suddenly turns tail and races back toward the lake. A fumble-fingered fisherman stumbles after it, slipping and tripping on slimy boulders and downed logs, trying to keep his line away from trees and alder brush as the fish scoots downstream, around a corner, and out of sight.

That's steelhead fishing.

Steelheading is fascinating for its contradictions. Most experts wield a fly rod and reel, but use no fly line and no real flies. They don't fly cast; they don't cast at all. And while their difficult but effective technique has homegrown roots, their quarry—the spectacular and glamorous steelhead—is an interloper, native to West Coast streams 2,000 miles away, no more a native to the North Shore than a mountain goat.

Those are not distinctions, however, that trouble my friend Shawn Perich, an outdoor writer who became an avid steelheader as a kid 20 years ago, after a steelhead snatched the worm he was drifting for spawning suckers. When the fish, far stronger, faster, and more acrobatic than

*Shawn Perich: Outdoor writer and avid North Shore steelheader.*

any sucker could hope to be, finally quit sprinting and leaping the length and breadth of the pool, it was tough to say which was more solidly hooked—the steelhead or Perich.

Still, success for Perich didn't come easily. It rarely does with steelhead. Mastering the strange art of "drifting" for steelhead (which really does resemble water dowsing as much as it does fishing) takes most anglers many fishing trips and sometimes several seasons. Perich and a boyhood fishing chum would fish Wisconsin's Brule River, coming home fishless even during that stream's glory years, when Brule regulars packed out a limit of five. "That really pissed us off," says Perich. But they honed their technique and the art of reading water until they hooked fish nearly every trip. Of course, actually *landing* these supercharged trophies was something else.

These days Perich lives outside Hovland, Minnesota, and drinks his morning coffee while admiring Lake Superior 50 feet away. The view framed by his front porch is occasionally interrupted by a timber wolf or moose. Today we watch the late April sunlight glint off the calm stretch of blue as we tie up spawn bags at the kitchen table, because Perich believes they're the deadliest bait to use when the water is still cold and the steelhead have just begun to move into the ice-fringed rivers to spawn.

We're hunkered over a plastic tub of fresh spawn, which Perich cut from the season's first ripe steelhead hen and keeps in the refrigerator, a habit tolerated—just barely—by his girlfriend, Vikki Elberling. Perich plucks a marble-sized lump from the sticky skein of bright orange-pink eggs, plops it in the middle of a two-inch square of pink bridal mesh, and closes the top with a few wraps of orange thread, which he ties off with several half-hitches or a whip finish (the knot used in finishing a fly or snelling a hook).

After I tie up a few bags, trout eggs are plastered to my fingers, to the scissors, and to the thread. "Do you have a spoon I can use for this?"

"Go wash your hands. You're doing something horribly wrong," Perich says. A strapping 220-pounder, Perich has the codgerly contrariness most men spend 70 years cultivating. "Don't crush them. You have to handle them real gently."

Hands washed, I try again. Within a half-hour, we have three dozen complete spawn bags apiece, which we dump in plastic spice bottles and sprinkle with just enough borax so they look like sugar-dusted hard candies. The borax preserves the eggs and soaks up extra moisture so they keep for days without refrigeration.

Perich often fishes a single spawn bag on a hook or uses one with a pea-sized puff of fluorescent synthetic yarn, the mainstay of North Shore anglers. Once the water warms to at least 38 degrees, he uses only yarn. "It's easier to fish and you can fish more aggressively," he says. "You can fish fast water, you can fish pockets, you can fish places where you snag on the rocks. I don't mind going through five hooks and yarn in 15 minutes, but I do mind going through five spawn bags in 15 minutes."

Elsewhere, steelhead anglers fish big nymphs, but rarely on the North Shore. "I'm a dedicated fly-fisherman," says Perich. "I'd prefer to catch fish on flies if it were at all possible. It works really well on the Wisconsin Brule, where there's a lot of insect life." But North Shore streams are far less fertile and rich in invertebrates.

Wisconsin steelheaders are more likely than Minnesotans to cast spoons, spinners, and crankbaits to spawning steelhead. The gravelly runs of the Brule are far more suited to that technique than the rocky pockets of North Shore streams, which snag plugs and hardware in an instant. "You lose a crankbait, you lose four dollars," says Perich. "I lose a hundred hooks, I lose four dollars. But in the time I lose a hundred hooks, I guarantee you I'll catch a lot more fish than you will on a crankbait."

We load our gear into Perich's truck. A few minutes later, we stand on the bank of the Flute Reed River. Warm sun on the snow-covered hills upstream has filled the stream with meltwater. Where we stand, less than a mile above the river's mouth on Lake Superior, it runs full, furious, and muddy down a string of low cataracts.

Perich reaches into the back of the pickup and pulls out a nine-foot, nine-weight graphite fly rod. "Graphite definitely revolutionized the sport," he says. "It not only made it easier, it also made it more glamorous." Nothing like tripling the cost of the equipment to increase the status of a sport. Steelheaders unanimously pay the price, however. The added stiffness and lightness of graphite, especially the latest "high-modulus" material, make the previously supernatural task of feeling rocks and the subtle takes of steelhead possible for mere mortals.

Many steelhead specialists custom-build rods with single-foot guides rather than the traditional wire snake guides. They feel that monofilament line slides through the single-foot guides more easily and the rod remains livelier and more sensitive. Perich, however, prefers standard snake guides, because he also uses the rod for regular fly-fishing.

His reel is the North Shore standard—a battered Martin 72. When you turn the crank, it makes as much noise as an old British Triumph. Perich likes it because the multiplying gear ratio takes up line quickly, and because it has the best inexpensive drag on the market. Any number of more expensive reels with good drags will also fill the bill.

Perich loads the reel with 10-pound test, abrasion-resistant monofilament—in this case, Trilene XT. (He also uses Maxima Chameleon.) If the Flute Reed were low and clear today instead of a roiled mess, Perich would slap on a spool of six-pound mono. Because mono stretches as you play a fish and reel in your line, it squeezes the spool like a rubber band wound around your finger. The mono can exert so much pressure that it spreads the flanges of the spool, ruining it. To avoid that problem, some anglers fill their reel nearly to the top with nonstretch 20-pound test braided Dacron, and top it off with 100 yards of mono.

Perich next snells his line to a number six nickled egg hook with an upturned eye (see sidebar). The snell forms a small loop between the hook eye and the knot to hold the yarn. Perich slips a fly box out of his pocket. Nearly all the sections are filled with different colors of Glo Bugs steelhead yarn, all cut to the length of a cigarette filter. He has Moss, Steelhead Orange, Shrimp Pink, Peachy King. One of his favorites is Oregon Cheese. He shrugs. "I just like the name."

## HOW TO SNELL A YARN FLY

The yarn fly is the most common, versatile, and effective lure for steelhead—as well as autumn-running Pacific salmon—in North Shore streams. It's simple and quick to tie, once you learn to snell monofilament to a short-shanked egg hook with an upturned eye. Here's how:

1. Thread the line through the upturned hook eye and form a loop that lies along the top of the hook shank. A 2-inch tag end should stick beyond the bend of the hook.

2. Pinch between your thumb and forefinger the front end of the loop at the hook eye. Use the other hand to wrap the loop around the hook shank and the mono that lies along it. Make at least five wraps.

3. Pull the tag end to tighten the front loop. Then pull the main line to tighten the rear loop.

4. Trim the tag end. Push the main line back though the hook eye to form a loop between the eye and the snell. Lay a short length of Glo-Bug yarn in the loop. (Perich often makes two-color

flies by putting two different shanks of yarn in the loop.) Jam the snell knot forward toward the hook eye and pull the main line tight to secure the yarn.

5. Trim the yarn with scissors to form a pea-sized "egg." Most beginners make yarn flies too big. To add spawn to the rig, simply hook the spawn bag beneath the knotted thread that closes the mesh.

Admittedly, the snell knot is tricky. Says Perich: "Some guy came up to me on the Root [in Wisconsin] and said, 'How do you tie that knot?' So I showed him. I just did one for him. Then I rigged up with my yarn and went back to my fishing. This poor guy and his buddy were on the bank for 45 minutes tying knots. Ruined their whole morning for them."

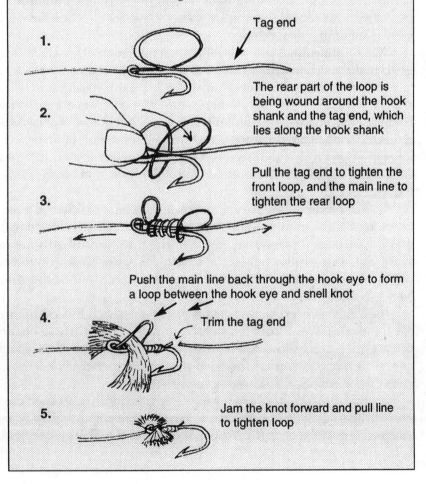

1.

Tag end

2.

The rear part of the loop is being wound around the hook shank and the tag end, which lies along the hook shank

3.

Pull the tag end to tighten the front loop, and the main line to tighten the rear loop

Push the main line back through the hook eye to form a loop between the hook eye and snell knot

4.

Trim the tag end

5.

Jam the knot forward and pull line to tighten loop

Like most steelheaders, Perich uses fluorescent yarn when the water is high and dirty; duller colors when streams are low and clear. He picks out a piece of Moss—a fluorescent green—slips it under the snell loop, pulls the loop tight, and jams the knot against the yarn, holding it snugly. Taking out a small scissors, he clips the yarn to within less than a quarter-inch of the hook eye, so that the fibers bristle out into a pea-sized ball. This is the egg fly. He finishes the offering by rolling a spawn bag out of his plastic bottle and hooking it through the nylon mesh, just beneath the knot of thread. Perich completes the outfit by clamping two number five split shot about 15 inches above the hook.

We scramble down to the river, a swirling brown sluiceway of yard-high falls, jumbled rapids, and foaming pools. Perich perches on an out-crop where the stream, only 30 feet across at its widest, plunges through a narrow notch into a swirling pool. Peering intently into the froth, he looks like a six-foot-tall heron in waders. Says Perich, "Steelheading is more like hunting than fishing."

What distinguishes stream steelheading from most other kinds of fishing is that the fish live in the lake and enter the rivers only to spawn, usually with the first gush of runoff in the spring. So if your timing is off, if the fish have not begun their upstream run, your quarry may quite literally be miles away and the water in front of you absolutely devoid of gamefish.

But the calendar, the warming weather, and the rush of meltwater all suggest to Perich that the steelhead are beginning their ascent. Now the trick is to guess their route upstream and ambush them where they're most likely to take.

As steelhead move upstream to spawn, they tend to follow the heaviest current without quite being in it. It's a difficult idea for a beginner to grasp. I point to a foam-covered eddy, which seemed fishy to me from years of chasing smallmouth bass in streams. "They're holding in the dead pockets," Perich admonishes, "but that's completely out of the stream. That's a cul-de-sac."

Instead, Perich explains as he traces pathways with his rod tip, steelhead move upstream through deep channels. Though these channels often appear to have the fastest current, boulders and other irregularities in the streambed interrupt the flow, allowing fish relatively easy passage through the envelope of slow water near the bottom.

Steelhead also follow "current seams," the boundaries between the fast current blasting downstream and the slower, more confused flow of water in an eddy or turbulence that rebounds from a cliff wall. These seams may be as crisp and obvious as a pleat in a new pair of pants or as subtle as the shadows in a Rembrandt painting. Yet they afford a migrating steelhead the opportunity to follow the main current—usually the most direct path upstream—without having to fight the full brunt of the river's grinding power.

Steelheaders also look for their quarry in pockets of calm water, where steelhead marshal their energy after ascending a grueling pitch of rapids or before taking on another. Steelhead are especially prone to lie in resting places on days like this one—when the water is cold and the fish are saddled with the lethargy dictated by their cold-blooded metabolism.

"Now maybe they're lying under that fast water out there," Perich says, pointing to the plume of current spewing from the notch. "There's quiet water underneath that. There's a quiet pocket in the center. There's a rock here and a quiet pocket in front of it and behind it."

"They also like this kind of spot," Perich says, pointing his rod to the gravelly fan at the tail of the pool, where the current gathers speed before plunging over the next drop. It's a real education to mark these places carefully and then come back in midsummer when low, clear water reveals the steelhead's resting places. It doesn't hurt, either, to carefully note where others are fishing.

"Just start working it, and I'll rock-hop and fish the far edge of the pool. We'll work this over for 15 minutes or so, and we'll know if there's something in here," Perich says. As an afterthought, he adds, "I've taken a 10-pound fish out of this pool."

◄ ◄ ◄

The "drift" is the key to North Shore steelheading, because these streams are too steep, craggy, and small to fish by methods common elsewhere. Try to troll from a boat as West Coast steelheaders do, and you'll fetch up on a rock in a capsized heap. Try to cast plugs and spinners as they do on Wisconsin's Brule, and you'll spend a fortune replacing the hardware you lose. If you fly-cast gaudy flies, nymphs, or streamers on fast-sinking lines, as they do on small western streams, your offering will pass far over the heads of bottom-hugging steelhead. And migrating steelhead, which are only marginally interested in food anyway, aren't likely to sprint upward through a jet of rushing current to snatch a passing gnat.

No, you have to put the lure—in this case yarn or spawn—on the fish's nose, even though the fish is burrowed into the riverine equivalent of a foxhole. Drift fishing is the best way of doing that.

Begin by pulling several feet of mono from the reel. Pinch the line in your left hand (assuming you're casting with your right) so that the lead shot hangs about 4 feet below your rod tip. Several yards of extra line should hang in coils from your left hand. Swing the lead from the rod tip pendulum-style, and release the line as you flip the sinkers upstream and across the current.

As the lead and lure drift with the current, take up slack by raising the rod tip. If the bottom is rather uniform, keep the rod at about a 45-degree angle, letting the split shot sweep across the streambed. If you have the right amount of weight, you'll feel an occasional tick as the lead touches rock.

## WHERE TO FIND STEELHEAD

Fish for migrating steelhead along the deep-water routes and current seams they will take upstream, or in the calm pockets just off the main current where they will rest between difficult pitches of rapids. The diagram shows several good lies and migration routes.

Look for steelhead to gather right below a steep rapids or falls (1), along the current seams (also known as "eddy lines") formed by a large boulder (2) and by a cliff or river bank (3).

Excellent lies form at the downstream end of midstream eddies, where currents converge (4). Also good are "tailouts" (5), where a pool or deep run becomes shallow and swift before sliding into a rapids.

Another steelhead highway is the current seam (6) lying between swift downstream current and the rebounding turbulence caused by boulders, riprap, or a rugged cliff along the outside of a river bend. Don't overlook the current seam (7) that forms between the main current and a large eddy on the inside of a river bend.

(Angler position rectangles show about where you would stand to drift through each lie. The locations will vary, depending on the depth, breadth, and swiftness of the stream.)

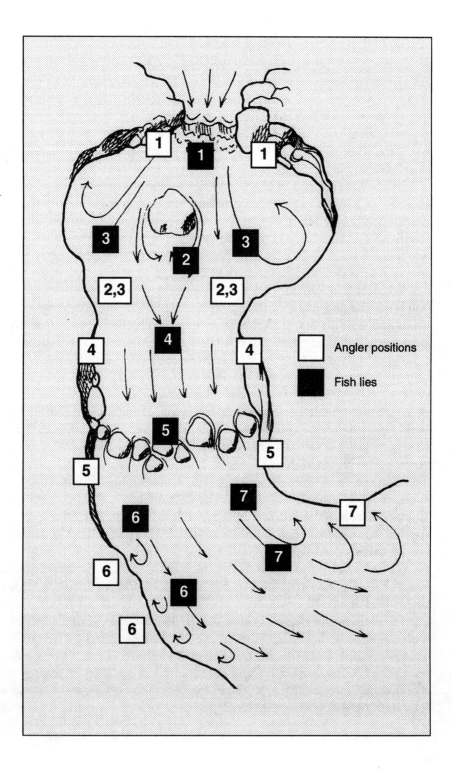

Angler positions

Fish lies

17

In more irregular runs, with dips and sudden rises, add enough weight so that you can feel the lead touch bottom as soon as you lower your rod tip. Then your task is to follow the drifting line with your rod tip, raising and lowering your rod as necessary to negotiate the underwater canyons below. You should feel the sinkers set down on the river bed at several points throughout the drift. "It's a hard concept to describe," Perich told me. "You're dead-drifting, but you're very much in control of your dead drift." Bring split shot—lots of it.

When the line comes to the end of the drift, let the lure hang in the current for a second or two, to give any fish that may be lurking there a chance to take it. Then, fling your wrecking balls back upstream, flipping overhand or under the rod tip as circumstances warrant. After a few tries, you'll figure out how to take in or pay out line with your left hand in order to control the drift and facilitate the flip.

You may also find, as I did, that after working a drift for a few minutes, you learn the geography of it and become more efficient, hanging up less often and needing less lead to stay in touch with the bottom. And after snagging a half-dozen times, you'll learn to avoid setting the hook every time your split shot touches a rock. In fact, working a drift for too long imparts a numbing tedium. One steelheader, Perich says, was fishing a swift, deep run from a six-foot-high cliff above the Brule River when he dozed off and tumbled into the rushing stream. Down he plunged into the dark, frothy water, traveling several yards completely underwater. When he finally popped to the surface, another steelheader shouted, "Well, did you see any fish down there?"

Warding off discouragement is tough for a beginner. The twisting currents are an unfathomable mystery. The drifting shot and yarn seem either to pass far above the bottom or fasten solidly to it. Often, there are no signs of fish. And the lure is unlike any other bait you've used, a fact that hardly instills confidence. Wondering if a steelhead swims within two miles of where I stand, I watch the neon balls of Moss yarn and orange spawn bob in the current and feel as though I've snagged Bozo the Clown on my backcast.

For perhaps the twentieth time, I flip the spawn bag into the troubled water against a rock wall, just below the gushing notch. The current swings my line downstream, the rod tip twitching as the sinkers touch rock. The line tightens at the end of the drift and, as I prepare to sling the works back upstream, I feel a double tug on the line, "Oh, man!" I shout. The line goes slack an instant later.

"All right!" cries Perich, who by now has moved to a spot about 30 feet downstream. "That means there are fish in here. He'll bite again. He'll probably keep biting until you catch him—unless he moves."

I drift again, and sure enough it hits again—a silvery fish that rolls and then disappears.

How'd you lose him that time?" Perich shouts.

Perich flings his rig into the run as I check my hook point and futz with my tackle. "He's just a little guy," he calls out, as a silvery form races around the pool. Minutes later a bright, 18-inch steelhead with the hooked lower jaw, or "kype," typical of spawning males, lies at Perich's feet. "We just hit the first fish in the river," he announces. "Definitely a wild fish."

◢◣ ◢◣ ◢◣

A steelheader's vocabulary is filled with confusing nomenclature that reflects the even more confusing history of this migratory trout in Lake Superior and North Shore streams. Wild fish, fin-clipped fish, 'looper, steelhead—all refer to fish of the same species but very different origins.

Steelhead are migratory rainbow trout, native to the western drainage of the Rocky Mountains. In recent years, biologists have changed their thinking about the rainbow and steelhead, reclassifying the species from *Salmo gairdneri*, a sibling of the Atlantic salmon and European brown trout, to *Oncorhynchus mykiss*. The change puts the steelhead in the same family as the chinook, coho, and other Pacific salmon, and acknowledges that the steelhead is identical to a fish that inhabits the coastal waters and rivers of Russia's Pacific coast.

Anglers recognize three varieties of the species. The rainbow is the resident trout of Western Slope rivers, spending its whole life in freshwater. The Kamloops is a deep-bodied inhabitant of some West Coast lakes. The steelhead, like the rainbow, spends its first one to four years in a river, but then swims downstream to the sea, where it fattens up on insects, crustaceans, and small fish for one to four more years, until it weighs as much as 20 pounds. Then the steelhead begins its arduous spawning run, a migration of as many as 500 miles to its home stream, usually a small tributary of a larger river. To make such a journey up rapids and waterfalls requires incredible strength and speed. Steelhead have been clocked at more than 20 miles per hour in short bursts and can leap six-foot falls with ease.

West Coast steelhead spawn mainly in spring, though some populations surge into streams during other times of year as well. Research indicates that steelhead stocks are genetically distinct from river to river, suggesting that the fish have adapted to the conditions along their migratory route and spawning stream. The prevailing streamflow probably governs the timing of the runs.

Because fish have adapted to their streams, many fish managers view stocking as a poor substitute for natural reproduction. It meddles in the fish's genetics and interferes with natural selection.

A steelhead hen builds her nest, called a "redd," on a shallow site where water wells up through gravel on the streambed. She rolls onto her side and, with powerful thrusts of her tail and body, excavates a shallow depression. There she lays her eggs, which are fertilized by attending males. Females typically dig several redds, excavating gravel from one to cover the eggs in the previous redd. The eggs hatch in about a month. Unlike other Oncorhynchids, steelhead occasionally live to spawn again and may do so several years in a row.

Long prized as a game fish, steelhead were first stocked in Lake Superior in 1895, in an era when fish managers engaged in a spate of enthusiastic experimentation that led to exotic and sometimes bizarre transplantations. Only a few years earlier, Spencer F. Baird, the nation's head fisheries manager, had given America the carp.

Steelhead took to Superior's clear, icy waters and began spawning in the lake's many tributaries—mere trickles compared to the streams their ancestors inhabited. A fish genetically programmed to swim hundreds of miles upriver eventually adjusted to a spawning run of 400 yards. Perich often fishes the Canadian shore of Superior, where a local once told him: "Take a piss in the spring and a steelhead will try to run up it, ay?"

Most North Shore fish spawn in spring, first entering streams in mid-April. Often, fish begin moving upstream as rivers rise from a spring rain or a spate of snowmelt brought on by a warm day. By the end of May, when rivers are usually returning to their clear summertime trickles, the run is nearly complete. Some fish, however, enter streams on a spike of high water in late fall and stay all winter to spawn in the spring.

Sometimes a straggler will surprise someone like my friend Keith Thomsen, a Duluth fisherman who eschews the hubbub of steelheading for quiet summer hours in solitude, spent fly-fishing for much smaller resident rainbow and brown trout. Once, as he drifted a Hare's Ear nymph through a low, limpid run, a steelhead the size of his thigh bolted out of a shadow and seized the fly. With only a three-pound test leader joining fish to fisherman, it was clear who had whom. Thomsen applied what pressure he dared, but the fish merely sulked in a pool. Finally he began heaving rocks at the steelhead to make it run and wear itself down. The tactic worked—sort of. His quarry bolted toward Michigan's Upper Peninsula, breaking Thomsen's leader.

It's unclear how much steelhead eat during their spawning runs, whether they be Homeric journeys up western rivers or sprints up Lake Superior streams. Apparently, some eat readily; others, not much at all. But they do pick up the drifting eggs of other steelhead and (in the case of fall-spawning fish) of spawning salmon. Why they do so is a mystery. Perhaps they do it out of the habit of eating, to gain nourishment, to destroy a rival's eggs, or to keep them from drifting into their own redds. "You'd have to ask them," Perich tells me.

For more than a half-century, steelhead stocking in Lake Superior was haphazard and slight. Steelhead survived largely unaided, adapting to conditions, reproducing naturally in their limited spawning habitat, and becoming naturalized, or "wild." But during the 1950s, when fishery managers viewed hatchery propagation as the solution to almost any problem, the Minnesota Department of Natural Resources began stocking steelhead in North Shore streams to satisfy anglers' demands for more fish. Since no one knew how many steelhead existed before stocking began, no one could say how much the stocking helped to boost the population. But the decade that followed, as any old-timer will wistfully recount, is still known as the golden age of North Shore steelheading.

During the 1970s and 1980s, however, anglers generally caught fewer and fewer fish for the time they spent on the streams. The reasons were varied and complicated according to Steve Hirsch, DNR fisheries program manager.

First, more anglers were sharing a limited number of fish, as fishing pressure increased by five to eight times. Not only did that mean fewer fish per angler; Hirsch says the increased harvest may also have cut into the numbers of wild fish.

Second, steelhead may have been losing out in competition with new species in Lake Superior. The accidental introduction of pink salmon in the 1950s created a burgeoning population of fish that may be competing with steelhead for the same invertebrate food. Coho and chinook salmon stocked by Minnesota, Wisconsin, and Michigan may also have taken food from steelhead, and they undoubtedly ate smaller steelhead as well. The ongoing recovery of lake trout, previously decimated by sea lamprey, contributed to further competition and predation.

Finally, Hirsch says, stocking itself may have worsened the problem. The genetics of steelhead that successfully adapted to their Great Lakes home may have been weakened by the haphazard introduction of new genetic stock that did not have to literally fight for its life in order to reproduce; a hatchery manager made sure of that.

Genetics weren't a major concern of fish managers when they first cast about for a remedy to declining steelhead numbers. They looked for a solution in the fish hatchery. What they found was a domesticated, easy-to-raise version of the lake-dwelling Kamloops, which they began stocking along the North Shore in the 1980s.

Though fish managers now worry that Kamloops are further eroding the fitness of naturalized steelhead, most anglers don't care. They love 'loopers because the fish are easy to catch on spawn and hardware as they stack up in the river mouths in late winter and early spring, in preparation for their spawning run. So, while fish managers would like to de-emphasize the Kamloops program, they often can't—anglers are as hooked on 'loopers as camp bears are on garbage.

Yet there's hope for a more environmentally sound steelhead program. DNR fish managers recently proposed a plan to rehabilitate populations of wild, naturally reproducing fish by the following methods:

• Restrict the number of wild fish that anglers can kill. The harvest will fall on "clipped fish," that is, stocked fish (usually Kamloops) marked by the removal of their fatty adipose fin.

• Stock steelhead fry with a proven track record in Lake Superior. Kamloops stocking will be restricted to the Duluth area, where it will be stocked to satisfy the masses who fish there. North Shore streams lend themselves to fry stocking because there are substantial rearing areas above migration barriers that are not heavily utilized by other game fish species.

Says Hirsch: "I'm pretty confident there's enough natural reproduction to provide a self-supporting population on the North Shore. I would, however, like to see a good source of Lake Superior steelhead fry developed for stocking."

◄ ◄ ◄

As winter loosens its grip on the North Shore, the steelhead run proceeds in fits and starts, depending largely on water temperature but influenced by rainfall, snowmelt, and other variables. In other words, timing is critical, impossible to predict, and a long-shot for someone who can't afford to fish every day. Catching a trophy steelhead—or *any* steelhead— is a matter of being in the right place at the right time. Savvy out-of-towners cultivate contacts among local fishermen and bait shops to get up-to-the-minute information. When the run is on, they drop everything but a fly rod.

Last weekend, Perich and two fishing companions hooked more than a dozen fish in the streams around Grand Marais, but today, just a week later, he and I have caught just the single fish on the Flute Reed. The unfathomable overseer of steelhead runs has apparently called off the party and sent the guests a-packing. So the hunt is on. We toss our gear in the truck and head down the Shore to the Brule. As Perich crosses onto the bridge, he slams on his brakes and peers upriver. "Damn seagull," he mutters. "If he sees me fishing on my spot, I'll never get on it again all spring."

The "seagull," he tells me, is an aggressive but not very knowledgeable fellow who finds it easier to spy on others than to find his own good runs and drifts. Actually, studying successful anglers—where they stand, how they cast—is a good tactic for a beginner to adopt. But don't expect the experts to like it.

"Let's fish here till he leaves," Perich says, walking to another good but generally well-known spot a couple hundred yards upstream of the spot where he really wants to fish.

I learned my own hard lessons about competition for scarce elbow room on steelhead streams 20 years ago on the Baptism—a crowded creek when a good run is on. I was fishing steelhead for the first time, using flies in a way I now realize was a long-shot. But as I swung a big white streamer through a fast run, a huge silver fish swooped out of a black shadow to snatch it but missed—barely. I cast several more times without a strike, then sat on the bank to ponder and rummage through my fly box. This was a fatal error. Growing up fishing uncrowded waters for bass, I had never experienced the rude ethics of shoulder-to-shoulder steelheading. No sooner did I plop my butt on a rock than a fisherman with a drift rig stepped between me and my potential trophy and flipped an orange ball into the head of the run. Seconds later, a gleaming steelhead popped out of the stream as smartly as a seed from a melon. Thankfully, Perich says, the streams near Grand Marais are uncrowded compared to the "combat scene near Duluth."

He puts me on the outside bend of the river, where the current washes past a series of boulders lining the bank. The resulting turbulence forms a seam about 10 feet out from shore, separating the "confused" water near shore from the rushing midstream flow. I begin drifting the spawn and yarn along that seam. I have just enough weight to feel bottom as I lower the rod tip—*tap, tap, tap*—and suddenly I'm stuck fast to a rock. No amount of jerking and jiggling dislodges the hook. (Careful—the only two rods I've broken met their ends when a hook was stuck on a rock.) I point my rod tip directly at the snag to avoid stressing the rod and tighten up on the line to break it.

Re-rigging spawn and yarn at the edge of a rushing stream, where the promise of catching a big fish surges as full and strong as the river itself, is as difficult to do well and in a hurry as, say, reloading a musket with a hundred enemy troops breaking over the ridge just ahead. It takes forever.

After an eternity passes, I flip out the yarn and spawn once again. *Tap, tap, tap.* Once again the same gremlin reaches out from under the rock and grabs the sinkers. Once again I break off.

By the third time, I have learned enough to lift the yarn and spawn over the offending rock and let them tumble back down into the depths once they're safely downstream. After a few more drifts, I begin to understand the mountains, valleys, and other geography of the drift and settle into an efficient rhythm: *Flip, tap, tap, tap. Flip, tap, tap. . .*

Hold on! The last tap pulls back and a big silver fish rolls on the surface a rod length from my feet. I try to keep the battle above the next set of rapids, but the fish races downriver, and I give it line. The river bends back toward my side and, as the steelhead courses around the bend, it threatens to wrap my line in the alders on the bank.

"You'll have to follow him down," Perish yells as he jogs down the riverbank, his landing net in hand. "It's shallow enough that you can make it if you stay next to the bank."

I stagger down the rapids, grabbing alders and stumbling over the shelf ice that still clings to the river banks. The fish ranges out and back across the river, 30 yards downstream. It never jumps—a fact I attribute to the icy water—but instead burrows toward the streambed until I apply enough pressure to make it move.

Perich slides into the river downstream. I finally work the fish toward him. He scoops it up and lays it on the shore ice. The steelhead is beautiful—iridescent violet flanks and olive back with the profile of a submarine. Perich stretches a tape along it. "Twenty-eight inches—a legal fish your first time out," he says in feigned disgust. "That's an eight-poι fish."

After admiring the fish for a few seconds more, I back the hook out of its lip, cradle it in both hands and slide it into the river, where it disappears in the stained water and becomes once again a part of the river.

◄ ◄ ◄

...ng down the volcanic escarpment that borders Lake Superior, Minnesota's North Shore streams are more beautiful than productive.

Soil is thin, and bedrock is never far beneath the surface, so these streams lack the steady flows of groundwater that nourish the best trout streams. Instead, North Shore streams depend largely on snowmelt and rain runoff, which cause cycles of flooding and drought. During winter low flows, ice may freeze to the bottom, destroying plant and invertebrate life anchored on the substrate. In summer, water temperatures may reach 80 degrees, high enough to stress resident trout.

The thin, stingy soils of the North Shore lack the nutrients and calcium necessary to buffer the naturally acidic runoff and produce a rich crop of aquatic insect life. As a result, North Shore streams support only about 30 pounds of fish per acre. Compare that with trout streams of southeastern Minnesota that flow over limestone soils rich in calcium and may produce 300 pounds of fish per acre.

Perhaps because of their shortcomings as trout streams, the North Shore tributaries historically held no resident trout and few fish of any kind above the steep falls that form a barrier to upstream migration from Lake Superior. In modern times, though, stocking has established self-sustaining brook trout populations. Stocking of steelhead fry is responsible for the many small rainbow trout that swim those reaches.

The lower reaches of North Shore streams, where a seemingly endless supply of trout could swim up to the barrier falls, presented quite a different situation. "Every river swarms, every bay is a reservoir of magnificent fish," wrote Robert Barnwell Roosevelt (uncle of President Teddy), who fished his way through hordes of lake trout, brook trout, and, surprisingly, smallmouth bass in Civil War days. Unfortunately, the gullible brook trout—especially lake-run fish of several pounds called "coasters"—soon became rarities because of overfishing. The proliferation of the alien sea lamprey in Lake Superior during the 1940s destroyed the lake trout population. The poisoning of larval lamprey in the streams where they spawn and the concerted stocking of native lake trout have put that fine game fish on the difficult path to recovery.

Shore-casters pitch dead tullibees, spoons, plugs, and even flies to catch lakers as they congregate at river mouths, especially during pre-dawn hours in late spring. In-shore trollers also do well near tributaries.

For a map of North Shore trout, salmon, and steelhead streams, ask for the free *North Shore Fishing Guide* from the Minnesota Department of Natural Resources, Information Center, 500 Lafayette Road, St. Paul, MN 55155-4040. You can also call 612-296-6157 or 800-766-6000.

# Chapter Two

———— ◄ ————

# BIG RIVER:
## *Down Here You Just Don't Know*

"Eat, eat!" Bob Nasby yells as he snaps out 80 feet of fly line as if he were shaking out a rug, dropping a deer-hair Dahlberg Diver within a few feet of the bank of the St. Croix River. "Eat!" Before he twitches the bug, a foot-long smallmouth snatches it and dances across the surface of the river. Nasby plays it out, then releases it. "I love smallmouth bass," he proclaims. "I love them."

A few casts later, I lay a big, black, rubber-legged fly against the shoreline. A solid hit, a big flash, then a strong run. The biggest smallmouth of the day? No. As I bring the fish to the boat, I see it's a three-pound sheepshead.

We're just beginning to sample the big river's variety. By the end of the day, we will have caught crappies, northern pike, rock bass, and a small muskie. And this was a slow day. By all rights, we should have caught a few walleyes and white bass.

Big rivers are the rainforests of the freshwater world, repositories of diversity holding an abundance of species unimagined by the angler who plugs a shoreline for largemouth or casts a fly for trout.

For example, standing in a single spot below the Ford Dam on the Mississippi River, I have caught more than a dozen different species: smallmouth bass, largemouth bass, walleyes, saugers, northern pike, white bass, crappies, carp, various suckers and carpsuckers, sheepshead, channel catfish, bullheads, and mooneyes. All these fish hit *flies*. Had I drifted a worm or fished a live minnow on the bottom, I might have added a dozen more, including flathead cats, gars, sturgeons, buffalo, and even American eels.

*Bob Nasby: St. Croix River guide*
*and fulltime fishing fanatic.*          29

The reason for this abundance? As a stream matures, growing from a riffling trout brook to a warmer and broader smallmouth bass stream to a deep river that may span a quarter mile, the character of the water becomes increasingly complex, offering a variety of habitat not found in smaller streams: extensive weedy backwaters, sandy bars, rocky shelves, cold spring holes, and scoured main channels more than 20 feet deep.

What's more, as a river grows so does the complexity of its food chain. A small trout stream may contain one or two species of trout, a half-dozen species of dace, sculpins, and other forage fish, and a few species of stoneflies, caddis flies, and mayflies on which they feed. On the other hand, a big warm-water river, such as the St. Croix or the Mississippi below St. Anthony Falls, is a turbid stew of life with more than a hundred species of fish and an infinite variety of plankton, insects, mussels, and other invertebrates.

None of this is lost on Bob Nasby, a St. Croix River guide and fulltime fly-fishing fanatic who fished from the river bank in Stillwater as he grew up. "If you listen to my mother, she'll tell you I never did," says Nasby, a one-time iron worker now in his fifties. "She'll say I didn't have a very good childhood, but I sure had a long one."

Back in the days when he fished bait more often, Nasby caught everything from bass to sturgeon to eels ("I don't touch 'em, though"). He was so impressed by this menagerie of fantastic creatures that he quite naturally disdained the walleye, whose virtues seemed puny and ordinary compared to the raw power of a big catfish, the beauty of a mooneye, or the athleticism of a smallmouth.

Such an attitude, as Nasby knows, is heresy in a state where the walleye is the state fish. "I could never understand what walleyes were all about until I brought one into shore and everyone goes, 'What a nice fish!'" he says. "And I was so impressed that they were impressed, I started fishing walleyes. I still don't know why I was impressed with walleyes, 'cause they don't fight good and I don't care to eat them."

Today we're not after walleyes, but smallmouth bass. We launched from a private marina just downstream of Stillwater and ripped across the placid surface of the St. Croix in Nasby's 90-horse Yar-Craft, a stable boat with seven-foot beam that he uses for tarpon and barracuda in the Florida Keys. Flanked by high wooded bluffs, the river runs more than a half-mile wide here through a long, slow stretch called Lake St. Croix. Though there is an obvious current near shore, the stretch is as much a lake as a river, with holes up to 90 feet deep. Now it's 10 A.M. Despite the beautiful, late-spring weather and reputation of the St. Croix as a highway of pleasure craft, I don't see another boat on the river.

Nasby runs upriver a short way before easing to within a hundred feet of shore. "Look down the shoreline," he says. "What you see is point, point, point, point, point." Indeed, that's true. The points are readily visible, each jutting just a few yards into the river. "I'm not worried about the water between the points," Nasby says. "I'm worried about getting from point to point. Most points are good for two to five fish. Then I move on."

With the bright sun, calm day, and relatively clear water, I can see the point nearest the boat fan into a shallow rocky bottom extending perhaps 60 feet out from shore and dropping quickly into the deeper water.

Often, Nasby says, fishermen make the mistake of racing in close to shore, spooking some of the biggest bass, which may lie just beyond the drop off into deep water. For that reason, we'll hang just beyond the breakline and cast Dahlberg Divers all the way in toward shore.

"That should do it right there," Nasby says, as I cast to a pile of rocks in shallow water. The Diver is a bulky, flashy fly with a cone-shaped, deer-hair head. About three inches long, it resembles the gizzard shad and other bait fish so important to the game fish in these big rivers. It floats at rest. I strip the line sharply a couple times to make the fly gurgle, then strip line in two feet at a time to make the fly dive and dart back toward the boat. After a couple more casts to the same area, I catch a one-pound bass. Simultaneously, Nasby catches its twin.

For the next two or three hours, we catch bass. Some lie up on the shallow shelf near shore; others ambush the lures as they dart over the lip into deeper water.

Because of its bulk, the Diver casts about as well as a shuttlecock. The prospect of tossing it beyond the breakline, the full width of the shelf, and all the way to shore—and doing so over and over for the entire day—would seem daunting to a less skillful caster than Nasby.

It's a problem, Nasby concedes—one he often contends with when he guides fly-fishing clients on the St. Croix. "If you can't cast, you can't fish," Nasby says. And by "cast" he means the ability to lay out more than 60 feet of line accurately and quickly despite a pesky breeze.

A good backcast is the key to good casting, says Nasby, who teaches fly-casting. "If the backcast falls apart, of course, the forward cast is done with." The loop formed as the line unrolls must be just as narrow and smooth on the backcast as the forward cast, he says.

"To steal a thing from Larry Dahlberg [the well-known fly-fisherman who designed the diving fly]—and I've stolen it for years—is to think of the water as a bucket of paint and the tip of your rod as a paint brush," Nasby says. "And you're thinking of a bull's-eye—and to flick that paint there," he says, looking at a target above and behind him for the backcast, "and to flick that paint there," he continues, looking straight ahead, where his line unrolls and lightly sets the bass bug onto the water.

Another hurdle to overcome is excessive false-casting, that is, casting back and forth to work line through the guides. This habit is particularly ingrained in dry-fly trout anglers, who use the casts to dry the fly and gauge distance. But on a big stream, a caster will wear his arm to tatters trying to false-cast a bulky bass bug with 50 feet of line beyond the rod tip. Better, Nasby says, to keep the line clean and coated with line dressing so that after the retrieve you simply pick up the last 20 feet of line, false cast

## IMPROVE YOUR FLY CASTING

More fly-fishermen would cast better if they realized that fly-casting is like working a yo-yo.

I came to this realization as I watched my young daughter. She'd let the yo-yo drop and yank hard, either before the yo-yo reached the end of the string or a fraction of a second after it bottomed out. Either way, the yo-yo died. Jerking harder didn't help.

Fly-casting is the same way, especially the backcast. Force it a bit too soon or too late, and the cast dies.

How do you know if your timing is right? Just as you do with a yo-yo—by watching the line and making sure it remains smooth, without shock waves traveling along it. The trouble is, when fly-fishermen make a backcast, the line is behind them, where they can't see it.

Here's a tip to help you watch and diagnose your forward cast and backcast.

Turn sideways to your casting target (as a batter stands in relation to a pitcher) and cast sidearm, with your rod parallel to the water (or the ground if you're practicing). As you make your backcast, you can easily turn to watch the loop unfurl. You can watch your forward cast with equal ease.

Strive to keep the radius in the loop small—what fly-casters call a "tight loop." The line should be smooth and free of any shock waves that indicate you're jerking the rod. Begin each casting stroke just as the loop unfurls.

once to work out a bit more line, then shoot the last 20 or 30 feet of line as needed toward your target. It pays to practice in your backyard, where you can experiment without the distractions of boat handling and fishing. There's no substitute for practice. Unfortunately, says Nasby, "We're a society of instant-gratification people."

⋈ ⋈ ⋈

When bass, white bass, northern pike, and other species of interest to Nasby seem to want a deeper-running fly, he often switches to flashy, light-colored streamers about the length of your finger. These he can work two to four feet deep. If he needs to reach deeper still, he may fish them on sinking line that will carry them up to 10 feet deep.

But fly-fishing isn't the only way to fish a big river, or even the most versatile way—not by a long shot. Spinning is. One of Nasby's favorite lures for smallmouth is a homemade stickbait that, like the Diver, imitates a darting bait fish. Nasby copied it from a bait he saw years ago, whittling it from a stick about four inches long and the thickness of a cigarillo. He installs a couple of light-wire treble hooks, and paints it green with a white belly. He fishes it much like a diver, except faster. He casts it into shallow water, lets it rest, twitches it a couple of times, then reels fast while switching the rod tip in 18-inch sweeps to make the stickbait dart erratically about a foot underwater. It all looks incredibly fast—like something he'd use for barracuda—yet the technique catches not only smallmouth but northern pike, white bass, and even muskies.

As the river warms in summer, St. Croix smallmouth—especially the large ones—spend more time in deep water. Nasby will fish shallowly with Divers and his stickbait at daybreak, but once the sun hits the water he moves out to where the flats and points break sharply into deeper water. He often resorts to six-inch grape plastic worms, rigged Texas-style or threaded on a jighead. Sometimes he substitutes a purple pork rind for the worm. Again, smallmouth may be the target but they aren't the only game fish to fall for jigs baited with worms or pork rind. Nasby often uses them to catch pike, crappies, and silver bass. Recently one of his clients, fishing a purple jig and pork rind, hooked a 20-pound buffalo.

The most reliable bait of all, Nasby says, is a white jig and minnow. "That's almost 100 percent dependable," Nasby says. He picks jigs from 1/8 to 1/2 ounce—heavier if he's fishing deep, or if the wind pushes the boat along at a fast clip. Consulting his depthfinder, he'll use the wind and trolling motor in combination to move the boat just beyond the break-lines. For smallmouth during much of the summer, he says, "17 to 22 feet seems to be the bite water."

He often finds crappies and walleyes a bit deeper, where a steep rocky or gravelly slope tapers into a flatter, muddier bottom. He may fish these areas with the same jig and minnow. Or he may switch to leeches rigged on a slip bobber, set so that the bait rides about three feet off the bottom. "Ironically enough," he says, "you catch a lot of gar that way."

The St. Croix also has big bluegills, which are more typical of lakes. (Rivers with extensive backwaters, like the Mississippi below Hastings, also hold large bluegills.) Nasby looks for them in protected bays where the current is slight, and fishes with wet flies or nymphs. If he's using spinning tackle, he'll fish a tiny jig below a slip bobber. Bait usually isn't necessary, he says.

These same dead-water areas are some of the best places to look for pike, which reach 20 pounds on a big, deep river like the St. Croix.

During the summer, as the water warms, big pike seek out areas where shoreline springs seep into a protected bay or pocket that collects the cold water. Pike with shoulders the breadth of fireplace logs will lie in surprisingly shallow water to stay cool. But these spots can be tough to find. "They're not boiling springs," Nasby says. "You can go right in where they are, and you can't see them. But if you try to wade in there, you'll find out where they're at. A dead giveaway is early in the morning when you see fog behind certain points. That's spring water coming up against warm air."

Nasby fishes these spring holes with spinnerbaits, buzzbaits, or big red and white Dahlberg Divers. "It's shallow water. You're talking maybe four feet."

A stealthy approach is critical. "You can't come roaring into the spot, pop the front seat up, and expect to catch fish."

◀ ◀ ◀

Though Nasby occasionally fishes with spinning gear, it's fly-fishing that he loves and that he'll try first under conditions even remotely suited to it. Even in the middle of summer, when Nasby suspects that bass are lying far down a drop-off in 20 feet of water, he'll patiently wait and wait and wait for a sinking line and streamer to reach a depth that a jig would attain in an instant.

Yet despite his devotion to fly-fishing, Nasby has never gone in for the sport in its classic form—casting dainty flies on wispy leaders to trout in a babbling stream. "Why can't I appreciate the serenity of those trout streams?" he asks. "I really like being on them. But the fishing . . ." Here Nasby pauses, at a loss for words. "Fly-fishermen tend to have an attitude. I've seen all this tweed and attitude."

And besides, he says, "It has no potential for a big fish. You know me, I'm a head hunter. *Big* means a lot to me."

So, instead of delicate trout in a dainty Midwestern stream, Nasby saves his fly rod for steelhead on the south shore of Lake Superior, chinook salmon on Lake Michigan, tarpon in the Florida Keys, and the grab bag called the St. Croix River, where the very next cast could bring the leap of a smallmouth bass, the lightning run of a northern pike, the jolting strike of a white bass, or—well, who can tell what might be next. "Down here," he says, "you just don't know."

## BIG RIVER MENAGERIE

With so much variety in big rivers, even an old river rat might have trouble figuring out what's on the line before it gets to the boat. And a lake angler may not have the slightest idea, even when it's flopping on the floorboards in front of him.

Here, for the uninitiated, are some of the species you're most likely to catch while fishing a big river for common game fish such as walleyes, smallmouth bass, and northern pike.

**WHITE BASS:** These small but feisty relatives of the saltwater striped bass roam big rivers in marauding schools. Their trademark is an absolute willingness to strike—and the strike is nearly always like a hammer blow, nearly enough to jolt the rod from your hands. A three-pounder is huge.

In the spring these fish push upstream into tailwaters below dams. Later, they scatter downriver and feed on shad and minnows, often in open water, but also along banks and sandbars. Wherever you find white bass, fish them with a small white jig, spinner, silver crankbait, minnow plug, or white streamer fly. Less important than the type of bait is its size and running depth. It should match the fish that the bass are feeding on.

As you fish, keep your eyes open for a patch of turbulent

water and a flock of screaming gulls hovering above: A pack of white bass has trapped a school of bait fish near the surface, and the birds are standing by to pick up the leftovers. Race over to the feeding frenzy, cut your motor to avoid spooking the white bass, and cast to the fish as you drift by the *edge* of the school.

CHANNEL CATFISH: These catfish are known for taking "stinkbaits" like chicken entrails, chicken livers, and other assorted dead stuff. But in clear water, you'll often catch them on the crankbaits, jigs, and streamers you use to cast for bass or walleyes. They put up a twisting, sub-surface fight with strong, bullish runs. Though channel cats can exceed 20 pounds, one to three pounds is typical.

Channel cats rest in deep pools during the day, but they move into riffles and dam tailwaters to feed in the evening. One of the best ways to catch them is to fish a large dead minnow or piece of cut fish on the bottom with a slip sinker.

FLATHEAD CATFISH: Unlike their channel cat cousins, flatheads rarely take dead bait. They prefer live fish. They don't often strike artificials. But when they do, you'll remember. Not only are they one of the most grotesque fish in the river, they're also one of the largest. One friend of mine was casting crankbaits for bass with a light spinning outfit when a flathead in the 30-pound range grabbed the plug. My friend did not mistake what followed for the fight of a smallmouth.

But catching flatheads on artificials is a long shot. It's better to rig a live sucker on a slip-sinker rig. Fish on the bottom of deep holes or near a tangle of sunken logs on a deep, outside river bend.

MOONEYES: If, as evening settles onto a big river, dimples appear all around as though you were on a trout stream, you may be in luck. Chances are the mooneyes are biting.

Mooneyes and their close relatives, goldeyes, resemble tarpon, except that they have small mouths and rarely exceed three pounds. Nonetheless, they strike at the surface and thrash wildly at the end of a line.

When the mooneyes are surface feeding, cover their rises with a small dry fly. If you're stuck without fly-fishing gear (which you should have with you, if for no other reason than the mooneyes), cast the smallest jigs or spinners you can rummage from your tackle box.

**CARP:** The carp's only sin is that, through no fault of its own, it's in the wrong place—that is, it's in the New World. If the carp had stayed in Eurasia, where it's native, it would be revered the world over as one of the gamest and craftiest fish in fresh water. Instead, because it has proliferated in this country beyond control, muddying lakes and streams and destroying fish and waterfowl habitat, we Americans despise the creature.

The surest way to catch carp is with light tackle (remember, it's one of the craftiest fish in fresh water), baited with a doughball or worm. Yet when a lot of fish are present, as in the tailwaters of a dam in spring, you can catch plenty on artificials. I like deaddrifting a small jig or bulky weighted nymph on a trout-weight fly rod. A five- or 10-pound carp may not run and cavort like a steelhead, but it surely does bend a five-weight rod.

**SHEEPSHEAD:** The sheepshead may get no respect, but it does have the greatest collection of nicknames of any fish that swims in Minnesota's big rivers. Among them: grunter, grinder, thunder-pumper, bubbler, gaspergou, silver bass, gray bass, and lavender bass (for its subtle but beautiful metallic sheen). In fact, "sheepshead" itself is a common nickname for this fish, which is more properly called the freshwater drum.

The sheepshead hits readily, strikes hard, and reaches more than 20 pounds (though one to three pounds is average). It also tastes good. In a recent taste test by a Wisconsin newspaper, it outranked walleye. Its saltwater relative, the red drum, is the basis of the popular Cajun delicacy, blackened redfish. Why more people don't fish for sheepshead is one of fishing's many mysteries.

Fish for sheepshead much as you would for walleyes—by bouncing jigs along the bottom. If the fish you bring aboard fights like a boot and has a milky eye, it's a walleye. If it pulls hard and grunts when you land it, you've got a sheepshead.

# Chapter Three

—◄●►—

# COULEE COUNTRY TROUT:
## *Going for the Throat*

Nothing quite so amazes an angler as watching an electrofishing crew go to work on a stretch of blue-ribbon trout water. Dozens of hefty browns, rainbows, and brookies—many far larger than anything the average angler has caught in years of fishing toil and torment—come twirling up from the dark recesses of the stream to the irresistible attraction of an anode charged with several hundred volts of direct current. Mere shadows on the stream bottom offer up a limit of keepers. A single downed branch holds three or four fish that, had they taken a dry fly, would fuel fishing stories enough to fill the off-season. From an inconspicuous cutbank comes a trophy that would win the local fishing contest.

A newcomer to the sport will bubble over with enthusiasm at the prospect of being turned loose on a stream nearly brimming over with 14-, 16-, and even 20-inch trout. But a veteran knows better; he has fished over all these trout without even seeing them, much less feeling their heft on his line.

Following Jay Bunke up a trout stream can be nearly as revealing. Bunke is president of the Trout Unlimited chapter in Rochester. We are fishing the South Branch of the Root River in June. I tried that stretch once before and decided it held few trout. But as Bunke marches upstream, plying the water before him with a fly rod, trout succumb to his nymphs and leap into the air like popcorn. The episode is every bit as educational as following an electrofishing crew—but with a difference. Watching Bunke pull fish after fish from the Root's racing waters, I know these fish can be caught on a fly rod. Thankfully, Bunke leaves a few for me to catch as I follow in his wake.

*Jay Bunke, pulling trout from the*
*racing waters of the Root River.*     39

"I used to agonize," says Bunke, providing running commentary as yet another fish bends his rod and circles his legs. "If I caught 40 trout in a night, I'd wonder why I couldn't catch 60. If I got a 16-incher, I'd wonder why I didn't get an 18. But I'm mellowing. It's like my father always told me, 'Geez, Jay, if you want to catch them all, let's just bring the net, scoop them out, and then we're done with it.'"

It's impossible to chat with Bunke for very long before encountering the rock-solid presence of his father, who shaped the course of his son's life as unmistakably as a sheer limestone bluff guides the path of a stream. Bunke grew up in Rushford, within a quarter mile of Rush Creek. "I remember catching trout in the 20-inch range on cane poles in town," he says.

As a teenager 20 years ago, he and his brother and father would roam the wooded valleys of southeastern Minnesota, hunting turkeys in the spring and fishing trout the rest of the year. His father remains one of his constant fishing partners and mentors. "I still learn a lot from him," Bunke says. Sometimes the two take turns as they fish, offering advice and encouragement as they share a single rod that Bunke built for his dad.

Bunke's long acquaintance with the coulee country of southeastern Minnesota is perhaps the reason he catches so many fish. As we work up through that first riffle on the South Branch, even as a steady parade of 10- and 12-inch trout inhale Bunke's fly, he casually says, "I still feel I haven't gotten the fish out of here I wanted." Incredibly, just minutes later, without having taken a step, Bunke announces, "There he is, there he is," and nets a 13-inch brown. As we wade up through another run and riffle, Bunke points to the slick but swift water just upstream, and explains that large trout resting in the pools often slide downstream into these "tailouts," or "slicks," to feed. In fact, between two large rocks lies a 14-inch brown, Bunke says, as the trout bulges the smooth surface of the slick to take a drifting insect. He points out three smaller fish taking insects near a cutbank on the left.

"Do you want to catch them?" he asks.

Stupid question.

"You've got to use your noggin to get a drift in here," he adds. "That's what makes it kind of charming." Since the biggest of the fish lie just upstream of the riffle, the fast water would rip the fly line—and consequently the fly—much faster than the slower water passing over the trout. The result would be to drag the fly through the water—a dead giveaway to wary fish.

"I usually come in from the side and do a good sneak on them," Bunke says, as we tiptoe through the riffle and move cautiously by the stream bank. Because the water is a bit cloudy from recent rains, he observes, "The fish aren't really spooky. To take those fish in August, you'll have to get down on your knees."

He hands me a number 12 Sparkle Dun, a stripped-down style he uses for much of his dry fly fishing. Unlike a standard mayfly imitation with a bushy collar of hackles at the head to float the fly, the Sparkle Dun consists simply of tail, body, and an upright wing. It's not as buoyant as other dry flies, but it works better on discerning trout in slow water, where they take a long look. This fly also had a twist: Its tail wasn't the standard two or three fibers meant to imitate the tail of a mayfly. Instead, it was a body-length piece of Z-lon, a bright, filamentous nylon. On the water, the fly looked like an emerging mayfly dun struggling to escape its nymphal skin. Trout, like other predators, have a fondness for disadvantaged victims.

I tie the fly on. "How should we attack this?"

"Hook your cast," he says. By that he means to cast a curve into the line, which will keep the line and leader off to the side, away from the fish. "The take will be really deliberate. Don't pull it away from him."

I make a dozen casts or more, each time afraid of casting too far and dropping the heavy fly line over the fish. Finally, I cast just far enough. As the fly passes over the spot where we last saw the rising trout, an olive form appears, turns, and slowly takes the fly. I lift the rod tip, bear down on the light leader, and follow the fish downstream through the riffle. Bunke circles behind me and nets the fish in an eddy. He holds it alongside the ruler marked on his own fly rod: 14 inches, just as he said, not an eighth of an inch more or less.

He lets the fish go, then points me back upstream to the three fish still rising near the bank. Taking much the same approach from the side and a bit downstream, I hook one after another. "Catching all four of them," Bunke says. "We should feel almost smug by now."

As effective as it was, the dry fly experiment was simply an interesting interlude for Bunke; he's soon back at work with his nymphs. "I dearly love nymph fishing more than anything else," he says. "I think what excites me most is how effective it is."

The reason it's so effective, as any experienced trout angler knows, is that rainbow trout of nearly all sizes and all but the very largest brown trout dine on insects. (Large browns primarily eat other fish.) And the overwhelming majority of these insects are in immature stages, living beneath the surface. To emphasize the point, Bunke fetches a rock out of the riffly water and turns it over. "These are immature *Stenonema*," he says, referring to a genus of mayfly abundant in southeastern creeks. "One is perhaps the smaller Gray Fox, the other the larger March Brown. Here comes a caddis," he adds, as a greenish wormlike insect wriggles out of a tubelike shelter of organic material and crawls across the underside of the rock. "Lots of flat-bodied, clinging-type mayflies. This guy's about ready to go. Look at his wing case—it's starting to separate here.

"The first thing I would do on any water I don't know very well would be to grab for rocks," Bunke says. "There's an amazing amount to be learned by not fishing."

When he does begin to fish, Bunke uses an eight-and-a-half-foot, five-weight fly rod with a double-taper line and a 10-foot leader. He ties on a 5X tippet today because of the murky water and relatively big nymphs we're using. If the water were clear and low, or if he were using small flies, he'd drop to 6X. His nymphs are slightly weighted with lead wire wound under the body. If the water is fast, as it is here, he pinches a tiny split shot (B or smaller) onto the leader, about a foot to 18 inches above the fly.

Bunke uses a standard nymphing technique of casting upstream and drifting the nymph straight downstream. The biggest failing of novice nymphers is not detecting the easy take of a trout intercepting the fly. To help see the take, Bunke pinches a small adhesive foam strike indicator onto the leader, near the knot to the fly line. "That way I don't have to change it when I want to fish a deeper run," he says.

(For those of us who *still* have trouble noticing the subtle twitch of an indicator located that far up the leader, I'd recommend a tiny Styrofoam ice-fishing bobber, smaller than your little fingernail. Slip it onto the leader and peg it in place with a piece of toothpick. Slide it down near the fly in shallow water and back toward the fly line in a deep run or pool. The distance from the fly to the float should be about one-and-a-half times the depth of the water.)

Bunke fishes with an economy of effort matched by few fly fishermen. He avoids excessive backcasts (the sin of many trout fly anglers) and keeps the fly in the water. After laying out a cast about 40 feet upstream and slightly across the current, he keeps his rod tip low, hooks the fly line over his right index finger and begins stripping in line to take in slack as the line, leader, and fly drift back toward him. When the indicator gets to within about 10 feet, he gradually raises his rod tip to lift the fly line from the water and keep it from "bellying out" in the current, causing the nymph to swing too fast through the water. As the fly passes downstream, he gradually lowers his rod. Finally, he points the rod toward the fly and, as if he were a fencer, thrusts in slow motion, to extend his drift by several feet. Thus, with a 40-foot cast, Bunke gets a drag-free float of nearly 70 feet.

"The first technique Dad taught me was the Leisenring Lift," he says. As the fly reaches the end of the drift, he lets the line tighten and slowly lifts the rod tip. The lift is named for Pennsylvania angler James Leisenring, who popularized it 50 years ago. It causes the nymph to swing upward as though it were a real insect swimming to the surface to emerge as a flying adult mayfly. Often, trout that ignore a drifting nymph viciously strike at one about to escape.

In clear water, Bunke often fishes to visible trout. But in the cloudy water we're fishing today, we spot few trout, and Bunke doesn't waste time fishing in peripheral areas. "When it's murky," he says, "I like to go for the throat to see if they've got the feed bag on."

The "throat," in Bunke's parlance, is the sweet spot, the prime lie that often gives up the largest fish. It's the very head of the run, where the shallow, food-producing riffle makes the transition into deeper, sheltering water. Here the largest fish in a pool will take up position when they're feeding, intercepting caddis fly larvae and mayfly and stonefly nymphs that tumble out of the riffle.

Typically, Bunke wades up the side of a stream, staying as close to shore as possible. He'll even stay on the bank if a stream is narrow and the banks are low and clear of brush. He'll begin peppering the run with casts, drifting nymphs down the middle of the run, along the edges, and even in the slack water or eddies that tend to form on either side of the run near the bank.

Bunke, however, pays special attention to the current "seams," the turbulent boundaries that form between the downstream-flowing run and the slack or upstream-flowing eddy current along the bank. Trout lie along these boundaries, taking shelter in the slower current while watching the faster current for drifting food. So Bunke lays casts to the current side of the seams, to the bank side, and right down the seam itself.

When fishing so many currents of varying speeds, you must learn how to "mend" line to keep the line, leader, and nymph traveling downstream together. If one lags behind—if, for example, the fly line catches fast downstream current while the leader and fly are in slower water—the line will drag the fly along, lifting it to the surface and making it appear as suspect as a powerboat in a yacht race. Line mending has become second nature to Bunke over the years. In fact, he talks of "using the current to get down into the sweet spots," meaning he is mending line to feed slack to the fly and split shot, allowing them to sink as deep as possible. As if to punctuate the remark, he sets the hook and leads another brown trout to his net. "Oh, life is good, huh?"

One run in particular proves challenging for a drag-free drift. The South Branch tumbles down through a swift riffle and turns a broad corner, carving a steep cutbank along the outside of the run while leaving a big, sand-filled eddy on the inside. The main part of the run and the current seam nearest us are easy enough to fish. In fact, Bunke and I catch several trout as we stand knee-deep in the eddy. But drifting a nymph down the current seam on the far side of the river proves nearly impossible. Surely some good fish are tucked up along the wall, but when I cast, the current grabs the belly of the line and rips the fly out of the slow water. I soon give up and concentrate on the easier-to-reach water in front of me.

"Does the term 'stack mending' mean anything to you?" Bunke calls out over the rush of water. He lobs his nymph into the seam on the far side of the stream. Then he roll casts several times. The casts are made at half-throttle—not vigorously enough to lift the fly from the water; just hard enough to stack several feet of loose fly line in a pile, right next to his strike indicator and above the sinking nymph. With all this slack line, the nymph can sink, even though the current may tug at the belly of the fly line. "Hopefully, you've got no drag," he says. "Everything's hanging straight down." After giving the fly several seconds to get down, Bunke takes up some of the slack line and fishes out his cast. The technique works; he pulls several foot-long browns and rainbows from the bank I had given up on.

In larger streams such as the South Branch, where delicacy and pinpoint presentation are not essential, Bunke often fishes two nymphs to speed up the process of learning what the fish are taking. But even if the fish vote solidly in favor of one fly, Bunke often continues to use both, in the hopes of appealing to a few nonconformists.

Throughout the day, he has fished a nymph called a Matt's Fur. Bunke uses it as a *Stenonema* mayfly imitation. First he wraps the bare hook with lead wire, and then mashes it with pliers to flatten it. The result is a flattened body that resembles the squashed form of mayflies clinging to the bottom of rocks. Then he dubs a body of tan otter and cream seal fur. He finishes the fly with gold rib on the body and a wing case of mallard or wood duck breast feather fibers (which are also used for a sparse tail). The tips of the feather fibers are splayed to the sides to form legs.

The *Stenonema* has proved a favorite, but Bunke continually changes the second fly in hopes of finding something that works even better. So far he hasn't.

We work upstream through one last run. This time it's Bunke's turn to

## HOW TO RIG TWO NYMPHS

Fishing two or three nymphs or wet flies on a line is an old-fashioned, highly effective technique. Fly fishers usually start with a long leader and tie short pieces of monofilament, or droppers, onto it. Then they tie the nymphs to the droppers. But this method is time-consuming, and the droppers often tangle. Bunke has solved the problem by simplifying the rig.

He ties the upper fly to the leader with a clinch knot, as though he were fishing only a single fly. Then he attaches a 16-inch piece of 5X or 6X leader material onto the eye of the first nymph, again using a clinch knot. He ties the second nymph, usually the heavier, onto the other end of the short length of leader. If extra weight is needed, he pinches a split shot on the dropper between the flies.

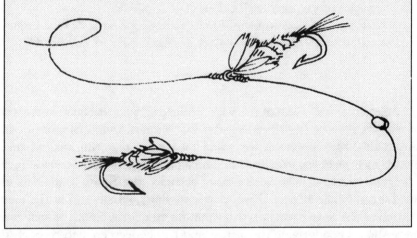

"go for the throat," so I cast to some fish rising in the tailout while he sticks close to the bank and heads upstream. As he begins working the head of the run, I watch him set his hook. Expecting to see a foot-long brown rocket out of the stream, I'm surprised to see that nothing seems to happen. Whatever is on the other end of the line doesn't move at all. Then Bunke's rod tip, already bent over in a hard arc, jerks downward as a big fish shakes its head, like a dog tugging on a stick. It begins to move around the pool. I can't see it from where I stand, but Bunke calls out, "Oh, yeah, I saw him. It's a good fish."

In a moment I see a flash. He's right. It *is* a good one. Moments later he leads it into the net, scoops it up, and tapes it: 17 inches, with big black and red spots, buttery sides, and broad olive back.

I notice the *Stenonema* hanging free on its dropper. "The other fly," I say. "What was it?"

Bunke's face goes pale, as though he's been caught in a horrible lie, and he looks down at the trout, wondering perhaps if there's still time to cut the line and let the fish swim free.

"I've got to talk to you about this pattern," he says, unhooking the fish and letting it swim into a quiet eddy to recover. The fly he pulled from its lip looks like nothing more than a small ball of black lint. "It's a pattern that an old-timer used to fish on Trout Run. He was like a grandfather. He actually passed it on to Tom Dornack." Bunke shakes his head. "Boy. I don't know if Tom would take exception to our talking about this or not. He tells other people himself, but he's one of those guys that . . . He's one of those guys."

"Not much there, is there?" I observe.

"Black fur and two wraps of black hackle," he says. "There comes a time in our season—about now—when it's damn near all you need."

◀ ◀ ◀

Minnesota has none of the wide, rollicking trout streams on the scale of the Madison or Big Horn or other big western rivers. Streams of that size in this state are much too warm for trout, supporting instead small-mouth bass, walleyes, pike, catfish, and a multitude of other species. In the miniature world of Minnesota trout streams, the South Branch of the Root is one of the largest. Down near Lanesboro, where it joins the North Branch of the river (which is too warm for trout) the South Branch is no more than a comfortable cast across and barely deep enough through the riffles, except in flood, to carry a loaded canoe.

At the other end of this spectrum are spring creeks, delicate necklaces of gurgling riffle and crystalline pools that sneak through tall grass and watercress and flow quick and cool in the deep shadows of overarching hardwood forest. Some are so small that you feel as if you're fishing in the middle of the woods, casting your fly into a distant bucket.

Of these dainty gems, one of Bunke's favorites is Gribben Creek, a three-mile-long stream where he recently fished for 80 days straight. The campaign—the "crazed 80," as Bunke refers to it—began as recreation, continued as experiment, grew into obsession, and finally ended as a return to sanity.

"Gribben was fishing really well that year," he says. "It was holding some big fish, and I was starting to spot them, which isn't always easy in Gribben. I would see some remarkable things. I wish I had time to do it again on any stream." If it weren't for his job as a technician monitoring employees' exposure to hazardous chemicals in IBM's Rochester computer plant, I have no doubt that he would do just that—repeatedly.

"I think you really get to see the personality of a piece of water when you're there day after day. It's almost like the great [insect] hatches know a weekend is coming, so they get it over with on a Wednesday and Thursday so the anglers never see them. On the 80th day I was just as concerned about whether I would catch fish as I was the first day I drove down there. I don't think I ever got to the point where catching fish was automatic."

By the 81st day, sometime in July, Bunke quit cold turkey. "I remember having the urge: I should go back. But, God, I had to stop somewhere. I could *still* be fishing the same stream." Then, as an afterthought: "It wouldn't be the worst thing."

We drive down Highway 16 out of Lanesboro, down the valley of the main stem of the Root River. By now it's a broad, riffly stream of genuine grandeur, its green bottomlands flanked by soaring bluffs, crowned by bald limestone outcrops. As we approach a bridge over a tiny tributary, Bunke glances in his rear-view mirror and slows to a walk. The tributary, he says, is the lower reach of Gribben Creek. "Ninety-nine times out of 100 there's fish rising." I look down and see rings spreading out from the center of the pool. Bunke spins off the highway and climbs the road leading up the valley of Gribben Creek.

The stream is tiny, small enough to step across in places. Looking into a pool, I can see every fleck of weed on every rock, and every conceivable place where a trout might hide. "Is it ever surprising when an 18-incher comes out of this," Bunke says. Accustomed to the size and turbidity of the South Branch, I feel like Gulliver tiptoeing through Lilliput, my every footstep thundering down the valley and sending all forms of life fleeing in terror.

"A nice fish rose up there, real nice," says Bunke, who has chosen to attack Gribben Creek with a two-weight rod and a leader tapered down to a 6X tippet to avoid scaring fish with line splash or a heavy leader. Many anglers feel it's impossible to land a large fish quickly enough with a light rod to successfully release it. Bunke disagrees. "Contrary to the debate that's raging over light rods, I feel I can land a big fish every bit as fast with this rod because I can really lean on him. It's almost impossible to break off."

He studies the river for a moment, but no insects rise from the water. "I'm not finding any clues right now," he says. "I'm going to run an ant along there." He rifles through a fly box and picks a number 18 foam ant and ties it to his gossamer tippet.

Since a bluff hems in the left bank of the stream, an angler will have to wade through glass-smooth water, or sneak along the bank and cast either left-handed or by reaching across his body with his right arm. It's enough to scare a right-hander to death. I stay put downstream while Bunke makes a few casts into the lower end of the pool. Satisfied that nothing is there, he tiptoes along the bank toward the rising fish.

When he's about 40 feet away, he squats and works out several feet of line, casting across his body and watching his backcasts to keep them out of the trees. He then lays out a cast that falls delicately to the water. The trout takes, and tears up the pool. Bunke nets it—a foot-long brown. Quickly he uses a small glass tube to evacuate the fish's stomach contents. "Yeah, ants and beetles in his stomach—about five different varieties. It's terrestrial time in Minnesota."

He casts again and takes a second trout, switches to a nymph, and gets another strike. Then, after many more casts, nothing. "That's the charm or disadvantage of a stream like this," he says. "Two fish—that pretty much does it."

The largest fish Bunke ever took from Gribben was a fat brown of nearly 19 inches. During the crazed 80, he caught remarkable numbers of 15- and 16-inchers and twice caught a 17-inch brown, each time in exactly the same spot. "I attempted on that fish at least two dozen times, and I caught it twice. You just don't know—a little bit of drag here and a bad cast there. The method I opted for was to start wading very, very slowly and stay in the weeds—putting my sneak on him that way. But like I said, about 22 times it didn't work."

The thick aquatic weeds that sprout in the clear, calm waters of a spring creek such as Gribben put a lot of anglers off, since working a nymph or other subsurface lure through them is nearly impossible. But Bunke uses the weeds to his advantage by switching to a dry fly, often a small cricket or other terrestrial. Hidden by the weeds, the trout seem willing to rise to the surface, even if no hatch is on. The result, however, is like fishing largemouth in the slop: Once the fish strikes, simply hang on till you get close enough to plunge your hand blindly into the weeds to retrieve your prize.

Without the security that weeds provide, Gribben's trout are often too skittish to approach at midday, Bunke says. "It's a morning and evening proposition unless you've got a hatch on."

Despite Bunke's initial success with terrestrials, we soon settle on small nymphs and work our way upstream. We cast them into the riffle at the head of each pool, and the trout seize them as though starved. Bunke lets his nymph drift a few feet, then twitches it lightly. "In some streams, that would put them off. In Gribben, they seem to like it. It must have something to do with their natural food."

The tactic apparently works. Bunke catches several trout in the 12-inch range and one 19-inch battler with a hook scar in its mouth. "A thrill like that is enough for me to believe in catch and release. Obviously someone left him for me," Bunke says, releasing the fish yet again.

Finally, near sunset, we reach a pool that's perfect in every way: A riffle enters, and the current sweeps around a right-angle bend with a cutbank on the outside and a patch of weeds on the inside. Boulders rest on the bottom and, best of all, several large trout mill about. Yet try as we both might—with nymphs, mayflies, caddis flies, and terrestrials—we drift right through the pod of whirling trout but entice none of them. We catch no more trout that evening, and it's almost reassuring to learn that there are things about the behavior of brown trout that even Jay Bunke doesn't fathom.

◄● ●◄ ●◄

## MAJOR HATCHES IN SOUTHEASTERN MINNESOTA TROUT STREAMS

| Insect | Time of Year | | | | | | | Pattern or Color | Size |
|---|---|---|---|---|---|---|---|---|---|
| | March | April | May | June | July | Aug. | Sept. | | |
| Ephemerella subvaria | | ▓ | | | | | | Dark Hendrickson | 12-14 |
| Baetis spp. | | ▓ | ▓ | ▓ | ▓ | ▓ | ▓ | Blue-winged Olive | 16-22 |
| Caddis | | | ▓ | ▓ | ▓ | ▓ | ▓ | Tans, olives, and some blacks | 14-22 |
| Ephemerella rotunda, E. invaria | | | ▓ | ▓ | | | | Light Hendrickson | 14-16 |
| Stenonema spp. | | | | ▓ | ▓ | | | Tan, yellow | 12-18 |
| Pseudocloeon (Little Yellow Mayfly) | | | | ▓ | ▓ | ▓ | ▓ | Pale yellow, olive | 20-22 |
| Little Yellow Stonefly (Yellow Sally) | | | | ▓ | | | | Dirty yellow | 12-14 |
| Trico | | | | | ▓ | ▓ | ▓ | Charcoal | 20-24 |

# TROUT AND TROUT STREAMS

Groundwater is essential to a good trout stream. Small creeks fed by runoff typically reach 85 degrees on a sweltering summer day—ideal for smallmouth bass, but too warm for any kind of trout. By contrast, on a 90-degree day, Gribben Creek will measure about 52 degrees near its spring-fed source and about 73 near its mouth, where incoming runoff has diluted the chilling effect of the spring water. Even a large trout stream like the South Branch of the Root, which takes in runoff from woods, farms, and sloughs in its comparatively large watershed, remains in the low 70s in the warmest weather because of abundant springs along its course.

Groundwater also brings in dissolved minerals such as calcium. These minerals buffer the natural acidity of rain water and increase the fertility and productivity of the streams. As a result, good trout streams support profuse aquatic insect life and an astounding number of trout, often numbering in the thousands per mile. Though trout are usually the dominant fish, most streams also hold chubs, shiners, sculpins, and various suckers, dace, and darters.

The colorful native brook trout (*Salvelinus fontinalis*) once swam wild in the cold-water streams of southeastern Minnesota. Most were lost during the late 1800s and early 1900s as farmers cleared land and drained wetlands, causing streams to warm, flood, and fill with sediment. Brookies also suffered in competition with the brown trout (*Salmo trutta*), introduced to U.S. streams from Europe in the 1880s.

Today, brown trout are the mainstay of the southeastern Minnesota stream trout fishery. The small brooks that line the state's coulee country sometimes offer up eight-pound fish, even though you can leap the narrow spots with a running start and a big pool is no larger than a Jacuzzi.

For years the Minnesota Department of Natural Resources sought to improve trout fishing by doing little more than stocking brown trout and limited numbers of rainbow trout (*Oncorhynchus mykiss*), both of which tolerate warm and turbid water better than the native brookie does.

During the last two decades, however, enlightened anglers and biologists have come to realize that wild, naturally reproducing trout, genetically adapted to their home streams, play an important role in a natural, functioning ecosystem. As such, they are far worthier beings than their pampered, pellet-fed hatchery cousins—even if they are a damn sight tougher to catch. So, despite the rantings of equally pampered anglers who are conditioned to follow hatchery trucks, the DNR has cut down on stocking and instead emphasizes stream protection and rehabilitation.

During the last decade, the DNR has also joined management agencies nationwide that have encouraged and required the release of trout in certain streams to permit the growth of trophy-sized fish. Most other states also ban the use of live bait in catch-and-release waters, because bait has been shown to kill up to 50 percent of the hooked trout. By comparison, flies and hardware kill fewer than 10 percent.

In streams with the right combination of forage and holding water for large fish, these trophy regulations do seem to produce larger fish. Despite the objections and second-guessing of politicians who listen to the hatchery-truck crowd, the DNR is continuing to experiment with special size limits and catch-and-release restrictions to improve the survival of big fish in streams that will support them.

To find the dozens of good trout streams that lace Minnesota's hill country, ask for the free map *Trout Streams of Southeast Minnesota* from the DNR Information Center, 500 Lafayette Road, St. Paul, MN 55155-4040. You can also call 612-296-6157 or 800-766-6000.

# Chapter Four

——————  ⊷  ——————

# TROPHY NORTHERN PIKE:
## *Getting Real Personal*

Up on the front deck, manipulating the trolling motor, Ron Kobes holds court in a voice at least as strong as Luciano Pavarotti's. Kobes brings the same intensity and enthusiasm to fishing that a SWAT team might save for bursting in on a gang of bank robbers with hostages. When Kobes talks about fishing, he does so in a tone of voice that you or I might use to address someone standing a quarter mile away.

"It really isn't the place for a two-piece rod—using heavy jerkbaits," he says, eyeing my light outfit with disdain. As he speaks, he rears back and lets fly with a Big Jerk, a huge jerkbait that looks like a billy club with treble hooks. With the trajectory of a Scud missile, it sails over 150 feet of Mille Lacs and hits the water. *Kerploosh!*

The huge lures he throws—most are about eight inches long—are muskie baits to most anglers, who use smaller stuff for pike. I mention this to Kobes.

"When I started throwing these big baits for pike, I noticed I caught as many small fish as I did when I threw dinky baits. So, why throw the small ones?" *Kerploosh!*

"You ever fish with spoons?" I ask, thinking of the big red-and-white Dardevles that anglers have flung and trolled for pike for decades.

"God made spoons to eat with, not to fish with." *Kerploosh!*

Kobes has a reputation for catching big pike and muskies. Perhaps you remember this television commercial from a few years back: Morning fog rises from a northern lake. A boat, far in the background, patrols the shore. A big plug arches toward the camera. A voice: "Crow Wing,

*Ron Kobes: A guide with a
reputation for catching big pike.*

Minnesota, means big northern pike." Jaws and teeth slash at the plug. The fight is on. A big pike is hoisted aboard. Next scene: fillets, lemons, and Old Milwaukee beer. "You know," says a fisherman, as he and his buddies nurse their bloated guts on the deck of a fishing lodge, "it just doesn't get any better than this."

I'm still trying to figure out where Crow Wing, Minnesota, is. But I've found out that the man who caught the big northern pike used in that commercial is none other than Ron Kobes. In fact, to get the fish needed for the commercial, he cast jerkbaits to take 17 pike from eight to 15 pounds from Gull Lake in less than three days, during a stretch of dead calm, hot, hazy weather in mid-June. It's just the weather Kobes treasures for pike fishing. The fish were lying in thick cabbage beds and darted out to kill Kobes's big jerkbaits. "It was just awesome," he says.

◀ ◀ ◀

A native of Austin, Minnesota, Kobes fell in love with fishing early in life and gravitated toward northern Minnesota, where he pursued walleyes, bass, muskies, and pike. In 1974 he started guiding. Soon after, he began fishing pike, muskie, and bass tournaments. "I do it for the cash," he told me when I first met him several years ago. "I ain't there for the show. I'm there for the dough."

Kobes had been recommended to me as a guide who could take me to really big northern pike, and back in the mid '80s I secured his services for a fishing trip. Trouble was, I hoped to take the pike on a fly rod. When I told this to Kobes, I expected to hear a groan of dismay. Instead, the challenge was met with what I learned was typical Kobes enthusiasm.

As we headed out, I remember asking him, "As a guide, what's your biggest nightmare, Ron?" I couldn't have known how ironic that question would be.

"Not satisfying my customers," he said. "My job is to give my client an enjoyable experience—a learning experience. It's unbelievable the number of people who think you go out and yank in 10-, 15-pound fish without putting any effort into it. Every morning you get a little twisting in your stomach, wondering if you can do it again."

Kobes guided out of Blackduck at the time, so we set out on Lake Winnibigoshish and searched out big submerged beds of cabbage, a broadleaved aquatic weed that attracts bait fish and, consequently, big pike. Once Kobes located a bed, he used his electronic depthfinder—one of the very first liquid-crystal graphs back in those days—to hold the boat just beyond the weedline as we casted back over the weed bed. At times it seemed as though we were a long way out from shore.

To make it short, the fishing stunk. Kobes threw jerkbaits and I laid down big streamers all morning. The payoff: one pike of about four pounds. "No sense in farting around," Kobes said. "I think we should go to another lake."

So we set off to Lake Bemidji, another of Kobes's favorites. And we fished the whole afternoon. Kobes picked up only two small pike, and I had nothing. I don't recall much about the fish, but I do remember one moment when I asked how deep we were fishing. Kobes looked at the depthfinder. "Five feet. No, four feet. Wait a minute. Do me a favor. Stick your rod in the water."

I stuck the nine-foot rod straight down until the water crept up the cork grip and wet my hand. No bottom yet. Suddenly the great, dark truth gathered up as ominous and unmistakable as a storm cloud and shot searing bolts of lightning through Kobes's confidence.

"The goddamn depthfinder doesn't work!"

The importance of this! His high-percentage spots might have been superb—if only we had been within casting distance instead of bobbing aimlessly in the middle of the lake with the gulls and pelicans.

Kobes, for his part, fell all over himself apologizing and stayed out on the water far longer than I expected as we searched gamely for more cabbage beds. I'm sure it was a sight he hoped no one would see: the guide at the tiller while the client leans over the bow, gauging depth with a fly rod. Finally, 12 grueling hours wore down our obstinate pride, and we motored back to the landing.

As I prepared to head back home, Kobes said we'd try again. Then he said—I can't quite believe he said it, but he did—"You know, Greg, it just doesn't get any tougher than this."

◄ ◄ ◄

"I have relived that nightmare many, many times," Kobes says now, sailing the Big Jerk out over Mille Lacs. *Kerploosh!*

"It was a fun day."

"For you maybe. It was not fun for me. Those are the days you wish you had a normal job."

Our strategy today is much the same. Only the depthfinders have been changed to protect the innocent—in this case, us.

It is late July, and we are following Kobes's typical summer pattern.

We begin by cruising the shallow bays on the west side of the lake about 300 yards off shore until the inky shadows on Kobes's Lowrance X-60 show the level bottom of the bay, typically 12 feet deep, rise rapidly to about eight feet. Where the breakline is clean, we motor on. But often, the depthfinder shows a thick wall of cabbage growing on the slope for hundreds of yards and extending in toward shallow water. The weeds typically reach to within a yard of the surface—just deep enough to be tough to see. So we rely on the depthfinder to define the boundaries of the weed bed. We move out about 20 feet beyond the deep edge of the weeds and begin casting back over the weed bed.

A good weed bed, says Kobes, lies next to deep water and is made up of the broadleaf pondweed most anglers know as cabbage. Unfortunately, many of the good cabbage beds are getting choked out by water pollution—sewage from lakeside homes and cabins that supports the growth of less desirable vegetation—"junk weed" in Kobes's words. Cabbage beds grow on hard bottom. If a few rocks and boulders are mixed in, the combination is super for big pike and, in a lake that has them, muskies.

Pike normally appear at these deep weed beds in early summer, attracted by yellow perch and other bait fish. The pike will spend much of their time in cabbage beds well into fall until the weeds turn brown.

As long as the weeds remain green, Kobes says, "then it's strictly daily weather patterns that will dictate where those fish are going to be—if they're going to be all the way in, if they're going to be on that outside edge, or if they're going to be out and away.

"If you have normal, stable weather, fish will be scattered all over. They'll be from the inside, to the middle, to the outer edge. They'll usually be up, meaning close to the surface.

"Now if you get into some frontal changes, some good temperature changes, those positions will change. A good velocity of wind will push some fish real shallow for a short time. The weeds will actually bend down and lay flat right on the bottom.

"Winni would be a good example. When that wind comes up and the cabbage starts laying flat on the bottom, you can go to that inside edge— sometimes four feet of water—and for a short time have some miraculous fishing. But it isn't something that's going to last throughout the day."

Cold fronts and the onset of cold, blustery weather cripple pike fishing, just as they do most other kinds of fishing. Yet, says Kobes, "sometimes you can have rotten weather, but if you have three days of it, it's stable. If you've got two to three days of it, no matter how rotten it is, you've got a chance."

Kobes's tackle would be familiar to just about any muskie angler. In fact, he uses the same rod, reel, and lures for both.

He casts a one-piece six-and-a-half- or seven-foot graphite rod made for lures up to two ounces. Though stiff, it's not the stout pool cue that many anglers use for working jerkbaits. Kobes has tried and rejected them. "I was just jerking hooks out of fish. They're just too stiff." To reduce the strain of retrieving big baits all day, Kobes encases the foregrip in foam pipe insulation and wraps it with electrician's tape. "It looks odd as the dickens," he says. "It'll actually form-fit your palm. You can fish with that all day long and you don't put any pressure at all on your hands."

On the reel seat, Kobes mounts a big ABU Garcia 7000 bait-casting reel, a veritable winch perfectly suited to light saltwater use. A pike or muskie would die of old age before it could swim off with even half the line a 7000 holds. Kobes likes the reel for two reasons: First, with the wide arbor and large capacity, the diameter of the spool remains large, even after a long cast, making fast retrieves easier. Second, the smooth gears and big crank make it easy to reel against the steady drag of a bucktail or big crankbait. "I use them and use them and use them," he says, "and I never have a problem." Kobes keeps the drag tight, but loose enough to slip if a big fish makes a sudden run at the side of the boat.

Still, it would take a hell of a run. Kobes uses 36-pound braided Dacron, which peels off a bait-casting reel smoothly on the cast and stretches hardly at all, transmitting the full force of the hook set to the fish's jaw. Such brute force isn't necessary with bucktails, spoons, and most other lures, but pike and muskies sink their impressive fangs into wooden jerkbaits so firmly, it's tough to break their grip to set the hooks. At one point, a big fish strikes Kobes's Big Jerk. He strikes back but misses the fish. Bringing the lure aboard, he says, "Look at that, teeth still in the jerkbait." I run my finger across the pitted wood and pluck out a triangular, white tooth tip.

Sharp as they are, those teeth will never stand a chance of slicing through Kobes's line. He ties off to a homemade leader that would be impervious to anything short of a cold chisel. It's made of a heavy duty swivel, about a foot of single-strand steel wire, and a heavy stainless steel snap. No component will break with less than 100 pounds of pull.

Now the bait. Kobes throws the usual assortment of lures usually meant for muskies: big bucktails, big spinnerbaits, and big diving plugs. But his first choice is always a jerkbait. He keeps one tackle box, which looks like a suitcase, just for jerkbaits, which hang by their trebles from plastic dividers. Nearly half are Big Jerks in a variety of colors: black, chartreuse, green perch, black and chartreuse, and black and silver. Second in number is Windels Muskie Hunter.

As much as he likes Big Jerks, he rarely fishes them straight out of the box. First, he touches every hook with a file so it's needle sharp. (By the end of the day, I had tiny nicks and punctures all over my hands from handling Kobes's baits.) Then he weights them so they dive deeper and stay deep, even during a slow retrieve. He does this by drilling shallow holes into the belly of the lure, near the forward hook hanger, and hot-gluing bullet sinkers into the holes. Fastened to a leader, the doctored plug floats more or less level with only the slightest bit of its back above water.

When he puts on a new plug, Kobes tests it by the side of the boat, looking for a deep dive and long side-to-side glide. If it runs erratically, he changes the action by bending the eye of the plug with a needle-nose pliers.

Angling literature is filled with the travails of muskie anglers who ruin their arms, backs, and shoulders by repeatedly casting and retrieving big jerkbaits. By season's end, they may as well be big-league pitchers, with bursitis, pulled muscles, bone chips, and dislocated shoulders.

To minimize stress, Kobes doesn't force the cast, but lets the long rod do most of the work. Once the plug hits the water, he gives a sharp, three-foot-long tug to make the bait dive. The depth to which it dives depends "on how big a pop I give it," Kobes says. Also, some jerkbaits, such as Suicks and Muskie Hunters, dive deeper than the Big Jerks Kobes usually uses.

Kobes always stands to retrieve the bait. (Working a jerkbait is nearly impossible while sitting.) He holds the rod by the foregrip, tucks the handle under his left arm and points the rod straight down the line toward the plug. He reels in slack and jerks the rod tip down to the water, moving the plug about two feet. He reels in slack while raising the rod tip so it once again points straight down the line. Then he pulls again. He falls into a steady beat, tugging nearly once a second. "Throwing jerkbaits—you get in the rhythm and it's not strenuous at all." Far more wearing, says Kobes, is a bucktail, with the steady drag caused by its big blade.

Once the leader nears the rod tip, Kobes sweeps the plug along the side of the boat, causing the plug to make a right-angle change in direction. "If you have a fish coming after it or following it, it's the last chance for the fish to make up its mind. If you change direction quick, it'll sometimes hit it."

Almost as soon as we start casting, we begin to see pike following our lures. "A fish rolled right there," Kobes yells. "I saw the white of its belly." Kobes keeps a second rod handy. It's rigged with a bucktail. He casts it to the fish that refused the jerkbait. Sometimes, the change in lure does the trick. Not this time, however.

Kobes picks up the rod with the jerkbait again. After a few more casts, he hauls back on the rod. Then the line goes slack. "I lost him. He really smucked it!"

"He really what?"

"He really smucked it."

Moments later, Kobes hauls aboard a three-pounder. A few minutes after that, his rod bows again, this time with a much larger fish. "Good fish, nice fish, nice fish," he says. After thrashing at the surface, it quiets down, and Kobes hoists aboard an eight-pound pike.

The pike are warming up. As we are about to find out, it just doesn't get any better than this.

## HOW TO LAND A BIG PIKE

Landing and releasing a big pike (or muskie) poses two serious problems: hurting the fish, and hurting yourself. Either is likely when a fish weighing ten pounds or more is swinging a plug with three needle-sharp treble hooks in the vicinity of your hands and major blood vessels.

Kobes solves the problem by carrying a needle-nose pliers, a Hookout (essentially a ten-inch-long pliers), and a landing net with a very wide hoop and a mesh bag big enough to sleep in. Also handy is a side-cutters for cutting hooks that are stuck someplace where they can't be removed (either in you or the fish).

When the fish is clearly played out, but before it is completely exhausted, Kobes leads it head first into the net. (This method works best with two anglers.) Then, *leaving the fish in the water,* Kobes works through the mesh with the needle-nose and Hookout to free the hooks. If possible, he releases the fish without ever bringing it aboard. Only if the hooks are deeply embedded or tangled in the net will he carefully lift the fish aboard and finish the procedure on the deck.

Two other items can make unhooking a pike easier and safer. The first is a heavy wire jaw spreader to keep a pike's mouth open as you operate on a hook lodged inside. The second is a pair of heavy leather work gloves that can take a lot of the abuse of working around sharp teeth and treble hooks.

Few freshwater fish have inspired the fanciful nonsense applied to the northern pike. A German pike skeleton that appeared in 1497 measured 19 feet long. A copper ring encircling its rib cage said it had been caught and released by Emperor Frederick II 267 years earlier. The "emperor's pike," however, never weighed the 550 pounds its captors claimed; it was a hoax, made from skeletons of several other fish.

In 1653, Izaak Walton wrote of a pike weighing more than 170 pounds that pulled an angler into the water and "doubtless would have devoured him also, had he not by wonderful agility and dexterous swimming escaped the dreadful jaws of this voracious animal." You'd think that Walton had been writing *Jaws* at the time, rather than *The Compleat Angler*.

It seems a fish of such prodigious qualities would engender great respect. Unfortunately, such is not the case. Big pike are still viewed as wildly destructive. Little fish, which snip off lures and occupy the attention of anglers who would pursue other species, are berated as "snakes" and "hammer handles." In Minnesota, anglers are still allowed to spear pike, a liberality rarely accorded game fish. In Vermont, in complete disregard for both sporting ethics and public safety, so-called sportsmen can shoot spawning pike with handguns.

In truth, northern pike are one of our most maligned and misunderstood fish. Several myths should be cleared up right away:

• *Big pike clean out the game fish in a lake.* Hardly. For one thing, truly large pike—the 20-pound monsters that anglers imagine ravaging entire populations of trophy-sized bass and walleyes—are too uncommon, even in virgin, unfished water, to wreak such destruction. Second, native fish have successfully cohabited with lunker pike for tens of thousands of years—and still do in remote wilderness waters and in some of the biggest and best fishing lakes in Minnesota.

Pike are destructive primarily after humans have tampered with the ecosystem. For example, the stocking of small pike in unnaturally high numbers—something the Minnesota Department of Natural Resources enthusiastically promoted in the past with the full support of anglers—can cause the forage base of a lake to collapse, crippling the game fish populations that depend on it. Another example: When the DNR—again, with the full support of anglers who can't leave well enough alone—stocks lakes with non-native trout and salmon, pike grow to leviathan proportions by slurping down perfecto-sized hatchery fish, whose ancestors never contended with the predatory instincts of the pike clan.

• *Having big pike in a lake will thin out the sunfish population and keep them from stunting.* Fish managers have found that big pike have practically no effect on sunfish populations. For one thing, sunfish are simply too numerous and prolific. In addition, with their broad, short shape, they are probably too agile in tight cover to be easily caught by a long pike, which is best suited for ambush in open water. Finally, pike prefer more cylindrical prey, such as tullibees and suckers.

• *Pike are hard to catch during summer's "dog days" because their mouths get sore or their teeth fall out.* A pike's teeth fall out all the time, but never *en masse.* They're continually replaced by others. And if a pike's mouth gets sore, it's probably from gobbling down spiny-rayed bait fish and smucking big jerkbaits. In reality, anglers have trouble catching pike in summer for entirely different reasons: (1) pike go off their feed if the water temperature in the depths they inhabit exceeds the mid-70s; (2) because suitably sized bait fish become most plentiful in midsummer, meaning pike are well fed and less likely to strike; and (3), most anglers fish too shallow in summer to catch large pike, which retreat to cool water—under 60 degrees if they can find it. And cooler usually means deeper.

Though the northern pike may not live up to the legends and myths many fishermen believe, it is an intriguing game fish. Above all, the pike is adaptable. It is the most widespread game fish in Minnesota, occupying nearly every lake in the state and most of the streams, except for the limestone creeks of the southeast. In fact, the northern pike (*Esox lucius*) is one of the most widespread freshwater game fish in the world, occupying the northern United States, nearly all of Canada, and Eurasia from the subarctic south to northern Italy and the Dead and Caspian seas. Other, similar species swim throughout the northern latitudes. The largest is the muskellunge in the upper Midwest, eastern United States, and southern Canada. Smaller relatives include several species of pickerel in the eastern United States, and the Amur pike in eastern Russia and China.

Oddly, *Esox lucius* grows significantly larger in northern Europe and the British Isles than in North America, though even abroad, none are large enough to swallow Izaak Walton's angler friend. The world-record pike—55 pounds, 1 ounce—comes from Germany, and several larger European pike have been reported. The U.S. record—46 pounds, 2 ounces—came from Sacandaga Reservoir in New York in 1940. Minnesota's record—45 pounds, 12 ounces—came from Basswood Lake in 1929.

A pike's long teeth are not only pointed but also have a knifelike edge to hold and kill prey. Built long and lean, with its fins and deepest part of its profile set to the rear for quick acceleration, the pike is capable of quick bursts of speed for ambushing prey. And its appetite is impressive. Pike often swallow fish a third their own length. An Irish pike reported to weigh 53 pounds was captured with a 30-inch salmon in its stomach. One 32-inch-long pike was caught with an 18-inch pike in its belly. And Canadian researchers working at the Saskatchewan and Athabaska river deltas put the number of baby ducks lost to northern pike at 1.5 million—nearly ten percent of total annual waterfowl production. To a large pike, Kobes's eight-inch jerkbaits are snacks.

Pike spawn in mid-March to early April when the water reaches about 40 degrees. They swim up marshy creeks or into weedy bays, flooded cattail marshes, and meadows. During flood years, pike have been found far from the main channel, stranded in pastures when water receded. The females deposit their eggs at random in water only six inches to three feet deep. The sticky eggs cling to vegetation until they hatch in about two weeks. Summer home development and shoreline weed removal has hurt pike reproduction in many Minnesota lakes.

Pike leave their spawning areas by April or early May. As the fishing season begins in mid-May, Kobes will cast spinnerbaits in shallow bays near spawning areas or along the first drop-off, where the bays lead to deeper water.

But as spring turns to summer and water warms, pike move to deeper water, taking up positions in deep cabbage beds and on deep, rocky points and shorelines. This is the time of year Kobes lives for, because the fish are active and accessible.

Some fish, however, remain elusive. Really large pike often suspend in deep water and feed on pelagic fish, such as tullibees. Unfortunately, these lunkers are nearly impossible to find. But in November, when water temperature drops to 40 degrees, tullibees begin to spawn, usually over shallow, gravelly shorelines or reefs. The huge pike that have shadowed them all summer follow them into shallow water. "Of course, they're up there for just one thing—to feed," says Kobes. So Kobes, in turn, shadows the big pike. "In the fall I'll start fishing bare rock," he says. He looks for reefs, points, and shoreline that break into deep water. And it's here he often catches some of his biggest pike of the season, fish over 20 pounds. He'll still give cabbage beds a good working over—but only if they're green. Once they turn brown, big pike abandon them.

Kobes has searched for those elusive open-water trophy pike with downriggers and lead line. He has caught a lot of fish, but few really large ones. Besides, he says, "It's not really my style of fishing. You have no chance to see a fish that doesn't take. Seeing a fish gives you a lot of different viewpoints—where that fish is setting up and how you're going to go about catching him. You're getting real personal here. You have a one-on-one hateship. It ain't friendship, okay? As a fisherman, that's what you want."

We cast toward shore, over a cabbage bed I can't see, though it shows up clearly on the depthfinder if we wander a bit too close. Although the depth remains relatively even, fingers of weeds reach out into the lake, perhaps as the lake bottom's hardness and composition changes. Kobes follows these uneven edges by moving shoreward with the trolling motor until he makes contact on the depthfinder and then backs out a few yards. Clouds of baitfish also appear on the screen. Probably yellow perch, Kobes says.

Two more ten- to twelve-pound pike follow Kobes's bait to the boat but turn away at the last moment. Then, just as I lift my jerkbait—a big black and silver Suick that Kobes just lent me—a pike of about ten pounds flies from the lake, spraying water over the gunwale. My first reaction, of course, is to rear back on the rod, ripping the plug from the fish's jaws. I'm left shaking, drained of all energy. The plug hangs a mere foot from the rod tip. The fish, of course, has disappeared once again into the green waters of Mille Lacs.

"What kind of release system is that?" asks Kobes. "Do I know how to tell you what kind of lures to use or what?"

Moments later another big pike follows Kobes' bait to the boat. Now it's his turn to be shaken by the experience. "How can you have that excitement trolling?" he marvels.

As though we weren't already agitated enough, Kobes soon gets another bump. This time, a big muskie—"in his early twenties," Kobes says—thrashes across the surface before throwing the plug at the boat.

Mille Lacs supports an increasing number of muskies, stocked by the DNR in ever greater numbers, to the delight of many anglers. Muskies never colonized Mille Lacs extensively on their own, which puzzles fish managers, since the fish do notoriously well in similar big, hard-water walleye lakes in the Mississippi River drainage, such as Leech, Cass, and Winnibigoshish. And the fish certainly are taking to their new home. "In the last two or three years, muskies have spread all over the lake," says Kobes.

"Has the addition of another big predator hurt the pike fishing?" I ask.

"Not as yet it hasn't," says Kobes. "The northern population is good, it's strong, and it's large." As I later find out, fish managers concur. So far, Mille Lacs pike seem to be showing no ill effects from competition with their close relatives.

Yet competition for food and cover would seem inevitable since the two fish (which can naturally interbreed to produce the infertile tiger muskie) eat the same cylindrical bait fish and occupy many of the same haunts. Muskies seem to prefer areas with reeds, rocks, and sand, Kobes says. Yet even after years of fishing for both species, he's continually surprised by which he catches next. By trial and error, he has learned that some cabbage beds, are good for pike, some are good for muskies, and some are good for both. But Kobes is often at a loss to explain what distinguishes one cabbage bed from another.

As if to prove the point, our big lures suddenly begin attracting far more muskies than pike. During the next several hours, I land a sevenpounder, and Kobes boats muskies of 18, 22, and 24 pounds. (The weights are approximate, since we didn't weigh them.) We both muff chances on similar fish, and a far larger muskie follows our lures to the boat several times.

"I'm fishing strictly for northern pike," Kobes swears, when I ask him if he's picking out muskie spots on purpose. "I'm not trying for stupid muskies."

Of course, Kobes doesn't really mind. And neither do I. The unexpected slashing strike and thrashing leap of a big muskie is just another bonus of Kobes's style of fishing on Minnesota's trophy pike lakes.

◄ ◄ ◄

If you can find tullibees, big pike won't be far behind, says Pete Jacobson, Minnesota Department of Natural Resources fisheries biologist in Detroit Lakes. Not only do these relatives of the herring provide ideal food for pike, but the cool water that tullibees need to survive enables pike to grow large.

Jacobson has examined the records of a long-standing fishing contest to find out which lakes have produced the largest pike over the decades. Then he examined the characteristics of the lakes to find the critical habitat they offer to trophy fish.

"Number one, you need some deep water," Jacobson says. "Number two, you need some cool water—deep enough and cool enough for tullibees to survive." In fact, a greater correlation exists between trophy northerns and tullibees than between big pike and any other factor.

Although yellow perch are important food for small and medium pike, once northern reach about eight pounds, they rely more and more on tullibees. Unfortunately for anglers hunting trophy pike, tullibees don't hang around cabbage beds or other easy-to-find structure. Instead, they roam the open water of a lake, searching for minute zooplankton. Tullibees feed heavily early and late in the day. Big pike pick off the tullibees from below—a task for which the pike is well suited, with its underslung lower jaw and ability to sprint.

Tullibees (*Coregonus artedii*) are common in many lakes in the northeastern United States and Canada. Silver in color, they reach lengths of a bit over a foot. They require cool, well-oxygenated water. Generally that means a deep lake, preferably with oxygen below the thermocline, or an exceedingly large one, such as Mille Lacs or Red Lake, which stays cool because of its size, despite a lack of deep water.

Trophy pike need these very same conditions, especially cool water, in order to put on weight. If water temperatures exceeds the mid-70s, as they often would in small shallow lakes, large pike go off their feed and lose weight. "As a northern gets larger," says Jacobson, "it needs cooler and cooler water."

# Chapter Five

◗◖

# SMALL-STREAM SMALLMOUTH:
## Action, Adventure, and Thrills

Dress Abe Lincoln in hip boots and fill him full of strong java, and you get an image of Tim Holschlag as he expounds on his favorite subject—big smallmouth bass and tiny creeks. Whether Holschlag just naturally has a manic glint in his eye, or whether it derives from his passion for smallmouth fishing, is tough to say, because ever since he was old enough to punch the button of an old Zebco, "crick bass" have occupied the eddies and pools of his stream of consciousness.

We've all read the ubiquitous "Small-Stream Smallmouth" magazine story in its various forms; Holschlag dismisses nearly all of them. "To most guys a small stream is where they can use only a four-horsepower motor on a johnboat," he says sarcastically whenever we get on the subject. "They can't use a 150-horsepower Gemini like Billy Westmoreland and blast around at warp-factor four with two trolling motors and a depthfinder."

No, when Holschlag says small stream, he means small—something too thin and skinny and crooked for a johnboat and four-horse. He means a creek you can wade across in hip boots, and better yet one you can skip across on rocks in the narrow places. In the years I've known him, he has taken me to streams far too small to be bass streams. They looked like brook trout streams gone warm. But we caught bass, plenty of them, and some up to three pounds.

He was reared on the fringes of the hilly northeast corner of Iowa and his fishing skill was bred on the creeks near home during the '50s and early '60s. He contented himself with creek chubs and green sunfish until

*Tim Holschlag: A teacher in the art*
*of stream smallmouthing.*

67

one day when he was about 10. "I caught this humongous, hard-fighting fish, which turned out to be a nine-and-a-half-inch smallmouth," he says. "The place we fished all the time wasn't much of a stream. It had about six bass per mile. It didn't take us long to figure out that if we took bass home, we wouldn't have the chance to catch them anymore. So we let them go and caught them over and over again." As he grew older and expanded the horizons of his fishing, Holschlag discovered more and better bass creeks throughout the Midwest—places where you wrestle with brush, fight nettles, rip your waders crossing barbed-wire fences, curse the fishing gods and, if you blink while walking, step completely over the stream.

Farmers and other rural folk in many areas didn't have access to lakes and reservoirs in those days, and they didn't mind walking. So they stalked the streams close to home, slowly drifting crayfish through the best holes—fast enough to keep them from crawling under a rock, slow enough to tantalize a big bass. Nowadays, anglers don't walk to fish; they'd rather stand on the carpeted platform of a big bass boat, the likes of which they see every weekend on TV fishing shows. Holschlag wants none of it.

"I enjoy being part of the fishing environment," he says. "I think you're as isolated as you can be sitting in a boat where you're not touching the water, you're not touching the ground, you don't feel the current. You might feel the G-forces as you race across the water, but you can't even hear anything that's going on because of the noise of the motor. I just enjoy the physical exercise and the physical sensations of wade-fishing a stream.

"You have challenging fishing with rapid, accurate casts on these small streams, and great fishing since you have lots of fish and probably have real low numbers of people, and lots of nature, things I don't mind sharing the stream with—deer, beavers, muskrats, kingfishers. I don't see how you can get that from many other kinds of fishing."

That's not to say Holschlag fishes only small creeks. He loves pristine lakes, especially the smallmouth and pike waters of the Boundary Waters Canoe Area Wilderness and Quetico Provincial Park, and the clear waters of the Sylvania Wilderness Area of Michigan's Upper Peninsula, where catch-and-release rules have allowed a fishery of huge and plentiful smallmouth bass to flourish. Holschlag even takes on the Great Lakes. In fact, he is the only angler I know who has nearly been killed by a smallmouth bass.

He was wade-fishing the fringes of Lake Michigan—a productive but little-known smallmouth hot spot—and casting as far out into the wide expanse of blue as he could reach. Like all of us, he suspected the biggest bass lay just a few feet beyond his range. Soon, Holschlag stood nearly chin deep in the lake, holding his arms high above his head to cast and retrieve the lure. He hooked a fish, a smallmouth of middling size that, as it turned out, had malice in its heart. The bass darted toward Holschlag's leg, implanting a sharp treble hook in his calf. The bass began towing its victim out to sea. Holschlag, luckily, had the strength—and still enough blood—to drag the bass back several hundred yards to shore, where he was finally able to unhook it and, magnanimously, release it.

The experience didn't sour Holschlag on smallmouth bass, but it couldn't help but to reinforce his love of small creeks.

><  ><  ><

I met Holschlag several years ago as we both fished the warm-water discharge of a power plant on the St. Croix River. It's the kind of desperate fishing northern river rats take up in February when all other forms of angling require an ice auger. As I pulled in a sheepshead, the fellow in hip boots next to me complimented me on my "lavender bass" and mentioned they taste every bit as good as walleyes and fight harder, too. In the Walleye State such a remark is close to blasphemy. I knew I'd found a comrade.

Not that Holschlag detests walleyes. He just detests walleye fishing in its typical form. "I like excitement. I like action, new adventure, and new thrills," he says. "When you fish walleyes and watch electronics, you've just about ruled out all of those things." Oftentimes, Holschlag has come across a school of walleyes in the deepest hole of a small stream and has proceeded to catch and release his limit within minutes by bouncing a featherweight jig or drifting a weighted nymph through the run as though he were fishing trout on the Madison. That's the kind of walleye fishing he can appreciate.

Trout, walleyes, saugers, white bass, channel cats, crappies, rock bass—all are fair game when Holschlag can catch them in moving water with light tackle. Since Holschlag renewed his interest in fly-fishing a few years ago, a favorite diversion has been taking a break from smallmouth fishing during the twilight to cast dry flies to rising mooneyes, a small-mouthed, herring-sized replica of a tarpon. And as October slips into November, and smallmouth slip into a coma, Holschlag often heads to a nearby small, sandy creek for northern pike. There, sneaking about dead-falls in his hippers and flicking spinners, jigs, or large flies into deep pockets as though he were fishing for big trout on a small stream, he pulls out pike up to 12 pounds.

But of all the fish that live in moving water, Holschlag loves the smallmouth best and often quotes James Henshall on the matter: "Inch for inch and pound for pound, the gamest fish that swims"—perhaps the most famous quote about a finned creature by an American author, excluding Herman Melville on Moby Dick. And of all the places to catch his favorite fish, the stream he loves the most is likely to be the one he is fishing at the moment, whether it's in the fertile limestone valleys of the southeast, the rocky pasture land of central Minnesota, or the coniferous and aspen woodlands of the north.

In some streams, smallmouth are year-round residents, migrating to deeper holes in the fall and moving upstream in spring to spawn. This seems to be true, for whatever reason, in small limestone streams in regions such as southeastern Minnesota, southwestern Wisconsin, and northeastern Iowa, where even large bass manage to overwinter in holes only four to five feet deep. In more northern locales, such as central and northern Minnesota, bass vacate small streams entirely with the onset of cold weather and water temperatures in the mid-50s. Though smallmouth have traditionally been thought of as homebodies, tagging and radio telemetry studies by the Wisconsin Department of Natural Resources in the St. Croix, Embarrass, and Wolf rivers have shown adult fish will sometimes migrate 50 miles to larger streams and deeper water downstream. If you're fishing perfect riffly water some clear, cool October day but can't catch a thing, the reason may be that there isn't a smallmouth of decent size within an hour's drive.

Otherwise, these small-stream smallmouth are like bronzebacks anywhere, seeking out reasonably deep water near current, with rocks or logs for cover. (Don't make the mistake I made when I first fished for smallmouth—concentrating only on riffle water; some of the largest bass in a stream often lie in slow-moving pools with plenty of woody cover.) These fish are eating opportunists, ambushing crayfish and minnows. By lake standards, they are ample but not huge. Holschlag's largest bass from a *small* stream was a bit shy of five pounds. A 14-incher (a bit over a pound) is big enough to earn an appreciative heft and admiring glance before he sends it back into the stream. "The size of fish is purely relative to what your expectations are and what your tackle is," Holschlag says.

His standard outfit is a seven-foot graphite spinning rod. "Light action is best for an all-around stream rod. A light-medium doesn't cast those 1/16-ounce lures as well. And you don't get quite the fight. If a 10-

inch smallmouth can't put a good bend in the rod, you've got too stiff a rod." Ultralight rods, on the other hand, "are just a little bit light. It takes a little more backbone to set the hook. Five-foot rods are just stupid. You don't get nearly the line control or casting ability. And you've reduced the hook-setting ability."

Holschlag uses a lightweight spinning reel loaded with limp six-pound test monofilament—four-pound if the water is really clear or the lures he's casting are particularly small. The lighter line allows better distance and accuracy. "A 1/32-ounce jig is a real beast to throw with six-pound."

To round out his tackle, Holschlag packs his fishing vest full of the following:

• Jigs, or as he often refers to them, "leadheads." He most frequently uses 1/32 ounce and 1/16 ounce. Anything larger has as much use on a small stream as a bass boat. "Never have anything in your box over 1/8 ounce," he advises. "If I were a teacher, I'd have a spot check for 1/4-ounce leadheads and take them out and give them to some lake angler."

• Spinner-flies. These lures, known sometimes as Cockatoush Spinners, must seem hopelessly old-fashioned to thoroughly modern in-fisherman types. Even in their heyday they weren't particularly well known. As *Sports Afield* angling editor Jason Lucas noted in the late 1940s: "One of the favorite lures of all really advanced and expert bass fishermen whom I know is a fly and spinner.... Strangely, its use seems to be confined almost entirely to the few experts; the average bass angler almost never uses it."

With the passage of time, the lure has become even less common—but no less effective. Holschlag, himself a student of the great Lucas, uses it frequently. He makes it with an Indiana spinner (about a number three), usually gold, connected by a split ring to a fly, usually a bushy, brown Woolly Worm. The beauty of the contraption is that it is nearly weightless (before the days of spinning tackle it was cast most often on a fly rod). Thus, he can coax it down through the thin waters of a small bass stream by increments, through the addition of small split shot about a foot above the leader. "It really cuts down on snags," Holschlag says. "The lead can be ticking the bottom and the spinner is riding up a bit above it." To make casting easier and more accurate, try putting the split shot right next to the lure.

• Tiny crankbaits. Tiny—like the streams. Holschlag's favorite is the smallest Rebel Crawfish (1/10 ounce). He also uses 1-1/2-inch Rebel Minnows. "Ninety percent of people never use something that tiny for stream smallmouth," he says. To fish these deeper, he sometimes pinches a

# TYING THE COCKATOUSH SPINNER

Commercially speaking, the Cockatoush Spinner is extinct. But it's as deadly as ever. Luckily, it's easy to make.

First, buy number three to number five Indiana spinners mounted on a short wire shaft. (For fly-rodding, try number one and two spinners for easier casting). Or, make the spinner assembly yourself from parts you can buy in any good tackle shop. Twist a loop in the end of a short length of .020 stainless steel wire. Slip on two small plastic beads (about 0.1 inch). Then add a tiny brass bead or a small football-shaped bead to help the blade turn more easily. Slip the blade onto a clevis and the clevis onto the wire shaft. To prevent line twist, add the smallest swivel you can find to the front of the wire shaft.

To tie the fly, start with a long-shanked number two hook with a straight eye (turned neither up nor down). Clamp the hook in a vise. At the bend of the hook, tie in heavy brown chenille and one or two brown rooster neck hackles (the wider and webbier, the better). Wind the thread forward to the eye. Wind the chenille forward and tie it off. Wind the hackle forward, being careful to not wind it over itself. Tie off the hackle and whip-finish the fly.

Finally, join the fly to the spinner assembly with a small split ring.

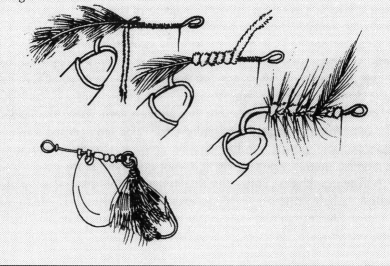

72

split shot about a foot above the lure. Also tucked away somewhere in Holshlag's vest is the all-time favorite shallow-running smallmouth lure, the floating 3-1/2-inch Rapala.

• Heddon Tiny Torpedo. The prop on the rear of this small floater makes as much noise as an old Triumph in need of a tune-up, drawing bass to the surface of slow-moving pools and eddies.

For a long time, Holschlag thought a fly rod was a poor substitute for a spinning rod. Then one evening, I coaxed three two-pound bass to the surface with poppers, from the exact spot where Holschlag has managed only basslets on jigs and spinners. Now he uses a five-weight fly rod as often as he does spinning tackle—not only for poppers, but small foam divers and sinking flies as well.

While Holschlag enjoys fly-fishing, he is unimpressed with most fly-fishers, including many fly-fishing writers, who seem preoccupied with intricate patterns and matching the hatch, which have little relevance to smallmouth. "A lot of them are great trout anglers," he says, "but when it comes to stream fishing for smallmouth, they leave their common sense in their other pants' pocket."

The problem, simply, is that many fly anglers try to trout fish for smallmouth, generally using flies too small and too light to interest a bass, whose feeding habits are far different from those of small and medium-sized trout. While a 12-inch brown may hold in a tiny niche in the current and rise to sip mayflies or drifting terrestrials off the surface of a stream, a smallmouth lies beside a boulder in an eddy, looking to pounce on a scuttling crayfish or darting sculpin. In fact, smallmouth feed much like large brown trout.

Holschlag appeals to smallmouth, however, with what he calls "weight-forward flies," which is clever sales talk for lightweight jigs dressed up as flies. The euphemism notwithstanding, I've used weight-forward flies for years with great success and always thought they made good sense. After all, if you're going to put weight on a fly, put it where it does the most good—on the nose, where it makes the fly sink like an Olympic diver and results in an attractive jigging action. Holschlag is keen on two such flies: One is a leech pattern made with a narrow two- to three-inch-long strip of rabbit hide and fur tied to the hook. The other is the Holschlag Hackle Fly, essentially a dark Woolly Bugger with a few bright rubber legs. He ties both on 1/32-ounce jig hooks. By doing so, he creates a fast-sinking fly with undulating action that's deadly on bass. But most fly anglers pretend not to notice how effective jig flies can be. They are too preoccupied dead-drifting small nymphs or stripping conventional streamers through riffles where only baby bass live to concern themselves with such effete offerings.

Because of these attitudes, Holschlag observes, spin fishermen often find it easier to make the switch to fly-fishing for smallmouth than die-hard trout anglers do. After all, he reasons, hardware-tossers have simply to learn how to fly cast and deal with new tackle. Trout anglers have the far more difficult task of shedding years of accumulated prejudices and misconceptions.

**◄ ◄ ◄**

As Holschlag and I fish, he soon leapfrogs by me and disappears around the upstream bend. About two hours later, he comes loping back with a vaguely sheepish look, like a springer that's been flushing wild, to report on news from the next county. (Usually he anticipates my largest fish and beats it by an inch and a half.) The man covers an incredible amount of water. Though I've not yet adopted his enthusiasm for chewing up miles on foot—his fishing trips resemble upland game hunting—his approach does pay off. He knows how to recognize bassy water, pepper it with well-placed casts, and pass up the empty water on his way to a new hot spot.

Usually, Holschlag moves upstream as he fishes a small stream on the theory that fish holding in current are facing upstream and won't spot his approach. Also, any sediment he kicks up drifts downstream, into water already fished. If the stream is small and the water low and clear, Holschlag will crouch low and creep along the bank to get into position to fish key locations, such as the head of a deep pool.

If he's using a jig or jig-fly, Holschlag casts upstream into deep water along banks, next to rocks and log jams, and into the runs where riffles spill into pools. With a jig and spinning rod, he keeps his rod tip high and the line just taut enough to bump the jig along the bottom as it drifts back toward him. He has become adept at detecting even light strikes. A lure that is too heavy will snag frequently, and to keep it off the bottom, the angler will reel too fast. So Holschlag uses a jig no heavier than he needs to reach the bottom.

If he's fishing a jig-fly and fly rod, Holschlag pinches a foam strike indicator—"the fly-fisherman's bobber," in his words—part way up his nine-foot leader. (The distance from fly to strike indicator should be one-and-a-half times the depth of the water.) Unlike a bobber, the strike indicator won't suspend a heavy fly, but it will clearly show when a fish strikes or the fly touches bottom. Holschlag usually casts a jig-fly upstream and nurses it down with the current.

When fishing a crankbait, spinner, or popper, however, Holschlag casts across the current and fishes the lure as it swings downstream with the current. This way, the current works against the lure, bringing out its action. But even when fishing downstream, Holschlag usually makes his approach from the downstream end of a pool or run, sneaking along in a low crouch if necessary and silently easing into position to cast.

Finding new fishing water is one of Holschlag's passions. On July days when the sun is hot enough to pop field corn, I've suffocated in the sweltering little compact Holschlag owns as he drives from bridge to bridge down dusty country roads and scrupulously scribbles in a big notebook he keeps—width of stream, clarity of water, amount of rock, depth of pools, and so on. Thankfully, we would scramble out of the car and fish if Holschlag found a stream to his liking, meaning generally a stream with some clean cobble and boulders, occasional riffles and a few pools at least four feet deep. Knowing that a small creek is a tributary to a larger bass stream is a big plus. (The stream survey files of the Minnesota Department of Natural Resources are a good place to hunt for smallmouth streams.) Every fish we would catch and release was recorded for posterity in Holschlag's same notebook.

The result of this homework and scouting is often surprisingly good smallmouth fishing. Holschlag's current treasure is a lightly fished creek only a few rod-lengths across that is brimming with 14-inch bass, which look mighty big in an environment that small.

Of course, exploration doesn't always pay off in the short run. "A lot of days I've explored a lot of miles of stream and haven't caught many fish, but that's the way you explore," Holschlag remarked one day as we set out on the Zumbro River. We had originally intended to fish a section of stream below the Zumbro Lake Dam, where special regulations require anglers to release all bass longer than nine inches. The result is a fishery of good-sized smallmouth. But in the cause of adventure, we changed our minds and drove instead to a stretch of water in the deep, shadowy Zumbro River canyon much farther downstream, where neither of us had fished for years.

This was big water for Holschlag—a good long cast across—so we used his lightweight aluminum johnboat. While I waited at the put-in, he drove off, parked his car somewhere downstream, and rode a little moped

# DYING SMALLMOUTH STREAMS

As we have polluted our streams with farm waste, farm chemicals, and municipal sewage, smallmouth bass have disappeared from many of the riffle-filled streams in southern Minnesota.

According to local legend, President Calvin Coolidge fished for smallmouth in the Straight River, the largest tributary of the Cannon River. Whether Quiet Cal actually made an appearance on the Straight is open to debate; that the Straight was once a superb bass stream is not. Its riffles and pools produced fish in abundance. Yet electrofishing surveys in 1974, '83, '84, and '89 turned up not a single smallmouth. Biologists are not sure why, but they suspect agricultural pesticides, which can poison fish outright, and organic runoff, which depletes streams of oxygen and smothers food-producing riffles and spawning areas with silt.

"It's too bad we can't get farms to run all their shit out through a pipe so everyone could see it," says Larry Gates, the regional watershed coordinator for the Minnesota DNR in Rochester. "No one would tolerate it."

Agricultural pollution of smallmouth streams is not unique to Minnesota. In southwestern Wisconsin, fish manager Robert Kerr has monitored oxygen levels in bass creeks to document the disastrous effect of agricultural runoff. According to Kerr, this organic waste supports a rich crop of algae, which produce oxygen by photosynthesis during bright sunny days and consume oxygen by respiration at night. The result: high levels of dissolved oxygen during midday and critically low levels just before dawn.

"The oxygen reading showed why bass don't bite at five or six A.M. in this area. They are probably in a daze," Kerr says. "I think that it would be very stressful for fish to be in an environment where the dissolved oxygen ranged from 18 parts per million to three parts per million in a 12-hour period."

Gully-washers make the problem worse. During one thunderstorm, one of Kerr's bass streams, Rattlesnake Creek, shot up four feet and turned into a muddy chowder. The concentration of suspended solids increased nearly 10 times. As bacteria broke down this organic soup, dissolved oxygen dropped to nearly zero. During the 12 hours after the storm began, most bass in the stream died.

back to the put-in.

The day was sunny and warm. Turkey vultures wheeled on the updrafts, and songbirds flitted through the bottomland forest. Billowing clouds overhead induced a kind of vertigo as we pivoted down the river like a leaf in the current. The first several miles of stream looked superb, with broad, swift riffles, long, slow pools, and deep, rocky eddies. But the habitat soon degenerated to a narrow strip of rocks along the outside bends as the rest of the river channel filled in with sand. Fishing was slow from the start. We caught fish up to 15 inches on artificials, but few of them. Holschlag even tried dredging deep runs and eddies with a jig and night-crawler, but he came up with nothing more than one of his lavender bass.

Once we passed Millville, the river turned completely to sand. It undulated beneath the boat like the dunes of the Sahara. For two miles we didn't even see a bass. When we reached the car, it was perched on a bluff, 30 feet above us, connected to the river flats by nothing more than a rocky goat path hemmed in by raspberries and sumac. I looked at Holschlag. Best he could find, he said.

Loading that johnboat was like trying to push it up over a house. Finally, we tied it off to Holschlag's bumper hitch and he drove off, dragging the boat up the bluff. As it reached the crest, the rope snapped. Thankfully, the boat jammed against some sumacs and my leg. Holschlag leaped from the car, grabbed the bow, and we wrestled the johnboat onto the road.

Tough work, but that's the price you sometimes pay to find good smallmouth streams.

◀ ◀ ◀

Over the years Holschlag has worked at various occupations, leaving most days free to prowl the banks of a creek. He now works as a freelance writer, sharing his knowledge of fishing in the pages of outdoor sports magazines and two books, *Stream Smallmouth Fishing* and *Smallmouth Strategies*.

As a writer, Holschlag finds himself in the bind of wanting to prose-lytize for his sport and yet keep his own fishing spots a secret. He is convinced that fishing pressure, more than any other factor, is responsible for the runty size of bass on many otherwise productive streams. The number of smallmouth larger than 15 inches per mile of creek—even in a superb stream—may total less than the number of clips on a stringer. On a good day, when bass are actively feeding, a procession of good anglers can make short work of those fish. "Some guys are just ceaselessly looking for a keeper," Holschlag says. "They feel happy just knowing how many fish they dragged home and killed." The result: The average size of fish in the stream plummets as big fish are cropped off and a bumper crop of young fish fill the niche. "If they just put them back, I'm convinced there would be good numbers of 13- and 15-inch fish on many more streams." Studies on streams with stringent size regulations seem to back him up, though Minnesota only recently began using such limits on state bass streams.

As for Holschlag's own fishing, according to his last tally, he has caught nearly 8,000 bass from waters moving and still, but "it's been at least 10 or 12 years since I kept a stream bass," he says.

Serious as the effects of overfishing are, they are temporary and limited compared to the damage wrought by pollution and poor land use. Several years ago, Holschlag walked the tiny creek he fished as a kid. "It was all shallow and silty. Pools that once were three feet deep were 12 inches deep. Marshes were drained and little woodlots were taken out and cornfields went in. The erosion seemed to intensify really dramatically. The water flow during the summer went way down because of the removal of the marshes. They would almost dry up during the summer." Plum Creek, as this upper branch of the Wapsipinicon was called locally, was not unique. All across the Midwest, Holschlag has discovered, many streams once teeming with smallmouth now support few or none. Some, according to fisheries biologists, were done in by pesticides; others by manure and other potent organics. The culprit, almost universally, has been agriculture.

"Farmers," says Holschlag, whose Iowa relatives nearly all tilled the soil, "have to be regulated just like any other polluting industry. No longer can they have complete disregard for what comes off their land into the water."

In reaction to the neglect and abuse of smallmouth waters and other warm-water streams, Holschlag and several other anglers in 1988 started the Smallmouth Alliance, which now has 250 members in several states. Holschlag cites two major accomplishments so far: First is simply drawing anglers' attention to the potential of warm-water streams and threats to those streams. Second is persuading the Minnesota Department of Natural Resources to enact special regulations on more than 80 miles of the Mississippi and Rum rivers, requiring anglers to release smallmouth in the sporty one- to three-pound range. "We're not going to be content to play with fewer and smaller fish—a dwindling resource," Holschlag says. "The

Smallmouth Alliance is actually going to try to turn it around."

Recently, Holschlag has channeled his love for smallmouth fishing into yet two more endeavors. He has begun guiding catch-and-release smallmouth trips, both on foot and by oar-powered johnboat. He also puts on day-long classes in the art of stream smallmouthing. His classroom is a small tributary of the Zumbro River.

"I enjoy streams and seeing other people learn about streams," Holschlag says. "Our streams need people who enjoy them, are very partisan towards them, and who really come to love these little ribbons of twisting, winding water."

◀ ◀ ◀

In most small streams, the key to locating smallmouth is finding clean rock and gravel, and water that is deep enough to provide security—usually three feet or more. Once you find such a place, (see diagram), here's how you might fish it:

Start by approaching the pool from the downstream end. While standing in the downstream riffle (or along the bank if the stream is very small) cast a small jig into the slick water just above the riffle (1). Active fish often feed in this swift, glassy water.

Move upstream along the inside of the bend. Provided the stream is no more than a comfortable cast across (50 feet or less), begin casting across to the lower end of the pool (2). This part of the pool is often too slow and filled with sediment to attract bass, so don't spend much time here. The downstream side of a downed tree (3) can be an excellent lie for large bass, especially if the current is strong enough to scour a deep channel and keep the underlying rock and gravel free of loose muck and sand. Make several casts near your feet as well, especially if you are standing on a rocky or gravelly flat that drops into deeper water.

As you move upstream, cast into the eddy on the inside bend (4), especially if it is 18 inches deep or more. If you can see the eddy is shallow and filled with sand, skip it.

Move to a position where you can easily scatter casts to the far bank. Toss a jig, spinner, plug, or popper just upstream of the downed tree (5) and tease it along the edge of the branches. The deep run sweeping down the outside edge of the stream (6) clears the streambed of sediment and often holds large bass. Cast a jig into the eddy behind the large boulder at the head of the run (7) and to the base of the riffle (8). The riffle itself is probably too shallow to hold large fish. (An exception: riffles of large streams, which are often deep enough to hold large fish.)

Finally, move to a position just below the upper riffle (angler position 9) and try a popper, spinner, minnow plug, or crankbait. Cast it to spots 5, 6, and 8 and work the lure back to you against the current.

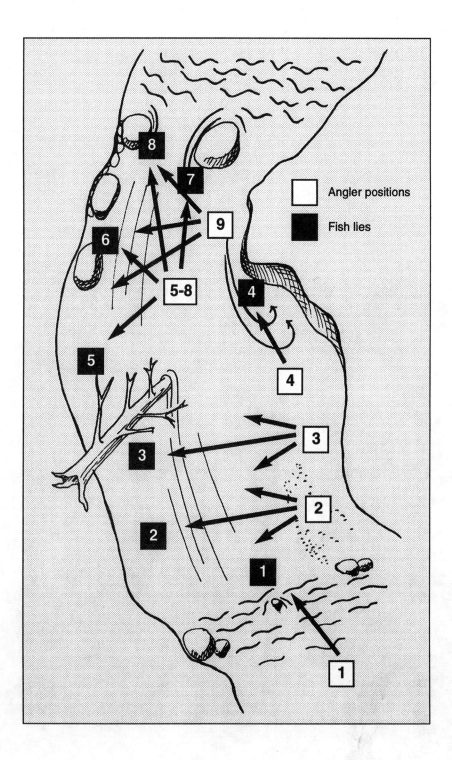

□ Angler positions

■ Fish lies

# Chapter Six

—◀—

# MILLE LACS WALLEYES:
## *Solving the Big-Water Riddle*

Bobbing in a wind-ripped Mille Lacs, we're surrounded by magic light, the brilliant halo that cuts through clouds and glimmers off the scallops of waves all around the horizon. The lake must have been a formidable beast to any fisherman—from the Dakota who huddled around its shores three centuries ago, to the sport anglers of 50 years ago—who all had to fear its stormy temperament. Yet today we charge into the hard east wind with impunity, my spine growing shorter each time we hit a three-foot wave. It's late May, but you'd think we were headed out to shoot bluebills. "I'm more dressed up than if we were duck hunting," Jeff Weaver shouts.

Weaver, a professional walleye angler, took second place the previous year in the Cabela's *In-Fisherman* Professional Walleye Trial. The man who took first, Dave Hanson, is running alongside us, a couple hundred yards away.

"Do we have radio communications today?" Weaver asks into a microphone.

"All clear," Hanson answers.

Weaver chuckles. "Another toy," he says to me.

For most of the week, the two fishermen have been scouting Mille Lacs for an upcoming tournament. Both Hanson, from Bemidji, and Weaver, from Anoka, have fished Mille Lacs—you could hardly call yourself a Minnesota walleye angler without having fished Mille Lacs—but neither has made a career of it. So today they are looking for spots and working out strategy. That's the challenge of a professional angler—to be a quick study. This week Mille Lacs, next week Lake Erie.

Weaver and Hanson fish from boats that, except for color, are identical: Lund 1775 Pro Vs—beamy, deep, V-bottomed boats. Weaver has rigged his with a 75-horsepower Mercury (tiller control), trolling motors fore and aft, and sophisticated electronics that just a few years ago may have been classified technology best suited to tracking down Soviet submarines. Nowadays, they're as familiar to serious walleyes anglers as a spinning reel. Besides the two-way radio, he has a liquid-crystal graph to show the depth, bottom composition, weeds, and fish. "Super unit," he says. "When we get out on the mud, you'll be impressed."

But most extraordinary of all is Weaver's loran, a receiver and computer that pinpoints a boat's location in relation to fixed radio transmitters on shore. (The name stands for long-range navigation.) Weaver and Hanson race from spot to spot across Mille Lacs, using their loran units to guide them. Some places they have known and fished. Others are unknown spots, gleaned from the new maps now being published that include loran coordinates.

At midday, Weaver motors up to Hanson just as he yanks a walleye over the gunwale. "There have always been fish—every time I've come here," Hanson says. The structure we're on is a "mud flat," a muck-covered plateau that rises about nine feet above the surrounding lake bottom. They are odd structures, apparently unique to Mille Lacs. Their foundation is a hard base of sand that rises above the bottom and is covered by a thick layer of organic goo. They are hatcheries of mayflies, midges, and other invertebrates. They provide fabulous fishing grounds for walleyes, especially during midsummer. Some are the size of a city lot; others stretch for miles. This one, like most, lies far out from shore, without a landmark to guide us.

"Look at all the fish up here," Weaver exclaims, looking down at his LCG. He punches the coordinates of the mud flat into the loran's memory. Then he and Hanson compare coordinates for another mud flat nearby.

Hanson: "46, 14, 46, 93, 41, 38."

Weaver: "I have 46, 14, 18, 93, 43, 46. How far is that off?"

Hanson: "The 14, 46 keeps you right in line with the longest part of the south end, and the 38 puts you almost on the southeast corner."

This is what fishing talk has become. Weaver enters Hanson's coordinates. The computer tells us we should go 1.31 miles at a bearing of 85 degrees. Weaver fires up the motor and the boat leaps from the water, speeding along like a computer-guided missile.

"It's getting to be more competitive on the fishing ground," says Joe Fellegy. "I'll see 14 boats out on the southwest corner of a mud flat. And they all have antennas for loran. They're making zoos out of my favorite fishing grounds."

In a state where the walleye is king, and Mille Lacs is the mecca of walleye fishing, Fellegy is the dean of Mille Lacs walleye guides. During the 30 years he took charter boats on the big lake, he became one of its best-known launch pilots. This notoriety he owes partly to his intense competitiveness, his enduring rivalry with other guides, and his consistent success in helping his clients catch limits of walleyes. And it derives partly from his curmudgeonly opinions—about fish, fishermen, and life around Mille Lacs—which he vents in a regular column in the *Isle Messenger* and in two books about fishing.

The more recent is *Mille Lacs: Thirty Years on the Big Lake*, an account of Fellegy's fishing and guiding experiences, from the day he first saw the 132,000-acre lake as a kid in 1950s until he quit piloting charter boats in 1989. "That came out of a kind of a reactionary spirit," he says of the book. "It has an attitude. It's a departure from this prissy, plastic fishing literature that's out there now. It's so uninteresting, so flavorless, so plastic. God, it sucks."

Fellegy has a slight build, sandy gray hair, and bookish mug with heavy-rimmed glasses. The tails of his rumpled flannel shirt hang outside his blue jeans. There's not much about modern trends in fishing he likes— not the least of which are the traveling medicine shows of fishing "experts" that populate the airwaves, magazines, and tournament circuit, bringing fishing expertise to every fumble-fingered amateur.

"As far as I'm concerned, the whole expert-pro thing has kind of screwed up the sport out there," he says. "I'm not attempting to be any kind of a purist—I mean I spent my whole life doing anything I could to get a fish."

It's just that fishing education—through magazines, books, videos, and seminars—has opened up the secrets of walleye fishing to anyone who cares to learn. "Everybody's writing about dirty-water walleyes and about early-spring walleyes and how to catch walleyes under this and that condition. And of course the grapevine is far more into the nitty-gritty now.

"Location has always been the big challenge," Fellegy says. "That has been turned upside down in recent years." With the advent of loran, just follow the experts, plug the numbers into your computer, and you've got a fishing spot for life.

This instant knowledge frustrates a guide like Fellegy who made his living by skimming the cream. "It's often important to get into a place first and get first crack at them—and get the dumb ones. What do you do when you go out to the south end of a mud flat where there's a nice little tip or a finger, where there's room for one or two boats—what the hell do you do now when you got 30 boats plastered on it, when you got 14 loran antennas bobbing there at seven-thirty in the morning? Where do you go in your charter boat? I'm very selfish in terms of spots. I like to be alone on a spot. Then you can work it the way you want. The biters—the dumb ones—are going to be yours."

And fishing knowledge further taxes a fishery already threatened by sheer numbers of anglers. "Imagine," says Fellegy, "for thousands of years the measure of success on the fishing grounds was coming in with the catch, coming into port with a bunch of fish. Now we've turned it upside down to the point of telling people not to keep a fish," he says.

"We need regulation. We need catch and release. But that is damage control and image control for what's going on out there. Tournament people are enshrouded with this conservation mantle. But they're the reason we've been driven to examining our conscience about keeping a fish. When there was only a handful of sharpies, there wasn't a problem. Mud flats were natural sanctuaries."

On a more personal level, the democratization of fishing has simplified the process of discovery and demystified local "sharpies," such as Fellegy. "One of the biggest satisfactions of the sport is doing the conquering and the figuring out myself," he says. "I want to be able to do that myself. I want to cross the frontiers. I don't want other people doing it for me. And if they do, I want them to keep their mouths shut.

"I love the challenge of the big lake. That's one of the big pluses of being on Mille Lacs—it is big and challenging and formidable."

◄► ◄► ◄►

Fellegy's challenge began in 1958, when he began guiding on the big lake as a 14-year-old. His schoolteacher parents had moved from New Ulm to start the Early Bird Resort on Mille Lacs' north shore.

The boats were round-bottomed and wooden, power provided in Fellegy's case by a spanking new five-horsepower Evinrude. The mud flats were a mysterious land beyond, truly accessible only to captains with their 30-foot launches, which could ride out the hard-driving storms Mille Lacs would unload on open-water anglers. To most anglers, "fishing the flats" meant simply fishing far from shore—a place where many dared not go except during the best of weather. "A genuine understanding of them resided only in the heads of a few launch pilots and fishing guides," says Fellegy.

Young Fellegy explored the flats, first in his wooden fishing boat, later in his dad's launch, an open boat more than 30 feet long. Fellegy found the sudden rise in the bottom by motoring along with a heavy sinker hanging from a stout fishing rod over the side of the boat. The advent of the first crude electronic depthfinders made the finding a bit easier, and bit by bit Fellegy began compiling a mental map of deep water, of flats, and of spots on the flats that often held fish.

Still, the depthfinder didn't solve the more vexing problem of pin-pointing the location of a fishing hot spot in a vast sea of rolling waves and bobbing gulls. With nothing more to guide him, Fellegy looked to shore for clues. Like nineteenth-century river boat captains who gauged their route along the winding spine of the Mississippi by studying the changing shape of the riverbank, Fellegy learned the landmarks he needed to guide him across several miles of open water to an invisible spot that might be no larger than a living-room rug.

In fog he often found his way by nothing more than a compass bearing and dead reckoning. Once, he started out from his place on the north shore, blinded by fog as thick as a cloud bank. He returned to the harbor three times. "I'd get a half block out and chicken out." Finally, he put his faith in his compass bearings and finely honed sixth sense of direction, and set off with a launch load of eight clients across the open water for a mud flat. "God, I hit the damn thing—near the edge, near the northeast corner, but I got it. Nobody there. By noon we were bearing down on the limit of 54."

It's early August as Fellegy explains how he navigates. We are trolling spinners and minnows across the mud flats a couple miles out in front of his house. We are aboard "the green turtle," Fellegy's weather-beaten Crestliner. You couldn't find a greater contrast with the sleek fishing machine of a tour-nament angler. The paint has flaked off of the wooden seats, and a crop of weeds springs from the dirt lodged between the seats and the inside of the hull. "I picked some of it the other day," he remarks. An 18-horse Evinrude pushes us along at trolling speed. The only thing electronic aboard is his depthfinder—an ancient Lowrance green-box flasher.

"Now I'll show you something," Fellegy remarks, directing my atten-tion to a tall tree off near Garrison, several miles to the west. As Fellegy motors north, the tree begins to merge into the hill behind it.

"Where's the tree now?" Fellegy asks.

"It just disappeared."

"Where that disappears happens to be right were this mud flat makes a bend," he announces, nodding to the green box for confirmation and dropping a marker overboard.

He points off in another direction. "There's a gap in the tree line."

"I see the gap."

"We call that the town line. It's the Malmo Road. If you go north or south very far, that cut isn't there. That's another navigating option, see?"

"How many mud flats are there?"

"Between 60 and 70. That's my guess. Who knows?"

"How does your mental map compare to the bottom-contour maps that show the mud flats?"

"Oh hell, I get absolutely no use out of those maps. All the maps published are way short of mud flats."

"Are you ever tempted to buy a loran?"

"I'd be frightened to death to be at the mercy of a piece of electronics," he says. "If the antenna broke or you had a malfunction or the signals were weak, suddenly the guy who depended entirely on electronics would be castrated."

◄ ◄ ◄

## MILLE LACS' MYSTERIOUS MUD FLATS

Since the late 1920s, when pioneering locals began exploring the middle of Mille Lacs, the big lake's mud flats have produced hot summertime walleye fishing, according to Joe Fellegy, who, in addition to being one of the area's most notable anglers, is also one of its most enthusiastic historians. But in all the years since, the origin of these unique and improbable structures has remained a mystery.

Mud flats are muck-covered plateaus. There may be as many as 70, Fellegy says, and nearly all lie in the northern two-thirds of the lake. Typically, they rise abruptly from about 30 feet of water and top out at about 22. A few flats near the north shore are only about 20 feet deep on top, but generally, the depths are remarkably consistent. Some are as small as a city lot; others stretch for miles. Some are long and narrow; others are circular; a few hook like boomerangs. No other lake in Minnesota is known to have anything like them.

A level plateau several feet high appears to form the base of each flat, says Tim Cowdery, a U.S. Geological Survey hydrologist who sounded the Mille Lacs basin during June 1992 with a special sonar designed to examine sediments and bedrock. These plateaus reflect all of the sonar signal, indicating they are probably made of hard-packed sand, Cowdery says.

On top of these plateaus—like thick frosting on a cake—lies a layer of organic muck, the remnants of midges, mayflies, and other invertebrates that have colonized the flats since the lake formed at the end of the last Ice Age more than 10,000 years ago, says Rick Bruesewitz, the Minnesota Department of Natural Resources' large lake specialist for Mille Lacs. This abundance of invertebrates provides a rich forage base for the yellow perch and other small fish on which walleyes feed. "It's not surprising at all that walleyes are attracted to the flats," says Bruesewitz.

What is puzzling is the origin of the sandy plateaus themselves. According to Cowdery, the sand was probably deposited or sculpted by the glacial forces that formed the basin.

Even stranger are the flat tops and consistent depths of these plateaus, as though they were all graded off by a giant bulldozer. One possible explanation, according to geologists: The level of Mille Lacs once stabilized at a much lower level than the present elevation, and the pounding of waves sheered off the tops of these sandy reefs at a consistent depth.

Cowdery hopes some of the mystery of the flats will be revealed soon, when the USGS will take core samples of the mud flats to more closely examine the structure of their foundation and measure the thickness of the overlying muck.

Not only did Fellegy learn his way around the lake, he also pioneered several walleye-catching techniques that since have become classics in the repertoire of serious anglers. As a "scrawny little book worm" with an inquisitive mind, he endlessly tinkered with tackle and varied techniques to catch more fish and gain an edge over other guides. As Fellegy now admits, as a kid he often violated daily limits to tote huge stringers of walleyes back to the dock to impress family, friends, and clients. "I wanted to be one of the best fishing guides on Mille Lacs, and I wanted to be one of the best navigators on Mille Lacs." Just because he now shuns tournaments doesn't mean he avoids going head-to-head. Every moment on the water was a contest in which he tried to boat more fish for his clients than other guides could, including his own father and younger brother, Steve. "I've always been highly competitive—ruthlessly competitive. That kind of competition is good, because it sharpens you and keeps you aggressive."

He despised complacency in the business of catching fish, and shunned the time-tested tackle and techniques used on the lake in those days: trolling with heavy braided line and steel leaders. "I can't stand this 'old-man' reluctance to change," he says. "I love old men on the fishing scene because they're fascinating to talk to, but some of them are not fast enough to change." That wasn't a problem for Fellegy, who experimented with the light tackle and monofilament that would become the mainstay of modern walleye fishermen.

Fellegy was fishing with a newfangled saltwater lure called a jig back in the 1950s, ripping it fast through the water in a way that wouldn't become well-known to other anglers for 30 years. He was "power trolling" with spinners and bait in the 1960s—again, nearly 30 years before the technique would catch on with the tournament crowd. "I'm famous for this spinner crap," he notes. Because of the warm weather and near calm, it's the method we're using today. "Spinnering generally comes into its own as Mille Lacs water temperatures warm into the mid-50s and warmer," he says.

Many anglers still use "crap and crud" and "heavy-metal garbage" — that is, spinner rigs with heavy, short leaders and big hooks, Fellegy explains as he rigs up the bait-casting rod I'll use. He rips open one of his own packaged spinner-leader rigs. Twelve feet of fine mono uncoil without a hitch. "I figured as long as they're spilling the beans, I might as well put a real one in a package." He now sells them at tackle stores all around Mille Lacs.

Fellegy perfected his spinner rig during long years of experimentation, using his clients as research assistants to find out which leader lengths, blade sizes and colors, and types of baits caught fish. The rigs we use today look like this:

• A medium-weight bait-casting outfit with eight- to 10-pound test line. The rod should be at least six feet long to better deal with the long leaders Fellegy uses. Beyond that, the particulars aren't important. When I ask Fellegy if I should string up my own rod or fish with one of his, he says, "No, use my garbage."

• A small three-way swivel. Tie the line to one ring of the swivel; to another, add a 10-inch, four-pound test monofilament dropper and heavy bell sinker. The dropper keeps the baits near but not on the muddy bottom.

"Walleyes aren't burrowed in the mud," Fellegy mutters. "Dragging this is like plowing rutabagas." Because we'll be fishing in more than 20 feet of water, Fellegy uses sinkers weighing nearly two ounces apiece to stay in touch with the bottom. In shallower water, he would use sinkers as light as 1/8 ounce.

• The leader. Fellegy uses six- or eight-pound test Berkley Trilene XL green. He's a stickler about avoiding kinks. Just a single curl is enough to cause him to tear apart a rig and retie. "If you have six-pound line and wrinkle it all up, it will have the visibility of 20-pound line," he says. Fellegy trims his own packaged 12-foot leaders to the correct length by first hooking the hook on the guide nearest the tiptop. Then he runs the leader down the rod, around the back of the reel, and back up to the tiptop. He cuts the leader a few inches shy of the tiptop and ties it on to the remaining ring of the swivel. Now, to store the rod, he reels the swivel to within a few inches of the rod tip, winds the leader down behind the reel and back up to the highest rod guide, where he hangs the hook. Rigged thus, my six-foot rod easily accommodates a leader of 10 feet. But why so long? "You'd have to ask the fish," Fellegy snorts.

• The hardware. The leaders we're using today are strung through a small metal clevis with a number three hammered gold Indiana blade. That's followed by a plastic bead with tapered ends (to help the clevis turn easily) and a half-dozen or more round plastic fluorescent chartreuse and pink beads to keep the spinner well forward of the minnow. Fellegy also fishes with silver, red, and glow-in-the-dark blades.

• The hooks and bait. Fellegy ties his own rig with two small short-shanked bait hooks, on which he impales a night crawler. My leader has a single number two light-wire gold Aberdeen hook with a straight (ring) eye. Fellegy reaches into a white five-gallon bucket holding rainbow minnows (northern redbelly dace) and "leatherbacks" (pearl dace). After sorting through a handful of minnows, he finally spies some barely perceptible trait in one rainbow, which is barely larger than a typical crappie minnow. "That one's got walleye written all over it," he pronounces. Without further explanation, he strings my hook in through its mouth, out through a gill, being careful not to damage the gill rakers. He turns the hook and impales it lightly through the back, just under the skin in front of the dorsal fin.

As Fellegy trolls at slow walking speed, I lower the rig into the water. The sinker hangs nearly straight down from the rod tip. The spinner turns as the minnow cocks to the side slightly and swims to stay upright. It flips to the side, rights itself, tips again, and finally is upright again. At Fellegy's directions, I lower the sinker until I feel it hit bottom; then I lift the rod tip a few inches.

For a long time during the 1970s and 1980s, the "pied pipers" of wall-eye angling touted slip-sinker leech rigs and dismissed spinners as old-fashioned "hardware." In just the last few years, however, tournament anglers have discovered spinners' deadly effect. "In modern parlance, it's called power trolling with spinners," Fellegy says. "It means moving fast enough to make the spinners spin, which means faster than the ultra-slow trolling with plain-hook rigs with leeches. I don't like the term because it implies speed trolling. It's not speed trolling. If you go too fast with spinners and live bait, your rig will twirl."

Trolling with heavy sinkers just inches above the bottom would be nearly impossible in lakes with jagged rocky bottoms. Even in the southern half of Mille Lacs, where rocky reefs and humps are common, we'd be hanging up or would suddenly find we're trolling far off the bottom. But the northern portion of the Mille Lacs basin is incredibly flat. It's the Texas Panhandle with water. And the flats are the flattest of the flat. Every so often I lower my rod tip to make sure the bottom is where I left it. Still there, give or take a few inches.

Moments later a fish hits, and I reel a small walleye aboard. "Sardine," Fellegy says. He quickly rebaits my hooks and carefully drops the rig over the side.

"You want me to do something?" I ask, feeing unaccustomed to being waited on.

"No, no, no. You watch your line."

Moments later, he hooks a larger walleye and insists I land it. Later still, I break off on a big fish. Fellegy races about the boat, retying the leader and muttering, "Down time, down time. It kills you." He has guided clients so long, he no longer simply fishes. "If I could just settle into being an ordinary fisherman," he says at one point, almost in exasperation. "I'm so used to pursuing this thing in maniac fashion."

Within minutes I catch a four-pound walleye and two more about half that size. Fellegy abandons crawlers in favor of minnows and begins to catch fish, too. "The night crawler and leech habit built up by the Lindners [Al and Ron, who publish *In-Fisherman*] caused a lot of people to forget the value of minnows," Fellegy says. Though, he acknowledges, "there are times you don't want a minnow in the boat."

Throughout the morning we motor from flat to flat, generally within a couple miles of shore. As Fellegy cases each new flat, he studies the flasher and looks for familiar landmarks. Satisfied he has found "the spot on the spot"—a particular feature that his yielded good catches in the past—he tosses out his marker. Then we begin trolling up and down within a couple hundred yards of the spot. Sometimes we troll on top of the flat, sometimes around the perimeter, sometimes back and forth over the steep slope in between. Often, Fellegy says, larger walleyes hang right on the drop. But today it seems to make little difference. "You notice I haven't been breaking my neck trying to follow the drop," Fellegy says. "But sometimes that's the best way."

Fellegy is convinced the mud flats always hold fish. "There's no question about fish being in those places I've had you today," he says. "We can wonder about whether they're active. When I come in here I don't know if they're going to bite. I might have a hunch that they will. But the thing is I never slide into a place like this thinking there aren't any fish. There are fish here all year. There's no reason for them not to be here." Oddly, many flats seem to hold more fish on the east side than on the west. "Why I don't know," Fellegy says. "It's a bit of a mystery, and it's not true of all of them."

While flats hold fish all year, they don't offer good fishing year-round or in all conditions. "On mud flats this time of year it's best to have it pretty quiet," Fellegy says, moving his hand along the horizon, as if to smooth the lake. The best time to fish them runs from about mid-June to mid-July, with the flats near shore getting better later in the summer. This summer, the bite has lasted a bit longer. "I think it's a function of food supply," he says.

"If you were here tomorrow with different conditions we might be doing something completely different," he says. With wind, for example, we might be fishing shallow reefs with Shad Raps or jigs and leeches below slip bobbers. Or we might find the fish turning on near the shore.

"If you throw a heavy south wind across some of those areas out there offshore, you'll just take a licking," Fellegy says. "But then the water might be dirty right up along shore practically, and those waves and the walleyes might be crammed in there like crazy. Of course, I'd wait for something like that. Before I'd even leave the harbor I'd gear up with lighter sinkers and be rigged for that shallow-water stuff. Go out on one engine. I wouldn't even bother starting the second one. The dog would be on shore wondering what the hell was the matter. The people would feel cheated because they didn't have a boat ride. Then we'd get right outside the harbor mouth and put the lines down and be tied to the dock at eleven o'clock with a limit for nine people. That comes from putting in your time."

As we move from spot to spot, we're joined by other boats—in Fellegy's words, "parasites," who don't know enough to find the good flats on their own. "You get one or two boats on here and then you can't work it right," Fellegy grumbles. "You're making all your turns according to who's there. The old men are the worst. They're the kind who push their way around a supermarket checkout line." For the most part, however, our companions will have to stick to the Safeway because they seem to be having rather poor luck on the lake. We even stop by to chat with the pilot of a big launch. With its long hull and open cabin, the boat looks like the *African Queen*. The captain ambles out of the cabin. Just a couple of walleyes, he reports.

Fellegy motors on toward the last mud flat. By now we're ready to quit. We've caught nearly three dozen walleyes, including several of about four pounds, most of which we released.

◖◗ ◖◗ ◖◗

After the 1989 season, after guiding on Mille Lacs more than 30 years, Joe Fellegy put his 34-foot charter boat into storage for good and quit the guiding business. It was a "wrenching" decision, he acknowledges, and he tried to make the final year stand as a monument to all the years that preceded. "That season I pulled out all the stops with all the smarts I had. That last year was the most satisfying I had in terms of outfoxing the fish—and the competition. The fishing was generally tough, but I did well."

Still, Fellegy—and the business—had changed. "That last year I could come home with a catch that would make a younger guide go crazy. He'd want to call the papers, he'd be excited, he'd be taking pictures. I was worried how long it would take to clean them. Would I get into town before the stores closed to get a case of oil? I noticed I was more hardened. Even when I got caught in bad weather I wouldn't get as apprehensive. I had been there before. When the fishing was tough, there were other things I'd like to do.

"I worked like a maniac from the time I was 14 years old till the time I was 46. Day in, day out, every day. Well, you only live once. There are a few things I want to do other than untangle an old lady's line."

Among these things is to write—especially about the history of Mille Lacs and its communities. "If I had to be jailed for a year and had one bit of recreation, I'd want a computer, a microfilm reader, plenty of paper, and access to my choice of old newspapers and periodicals."

He has also capitalized on his own notoriety and the angling public's thirst for fishing information by writing and publishing *Joe Fellegy's Mille Lacs Fishing Digest*, a quarterly tabloid that covers the fishing scene on the big lake, from tackle and techniques to angler profiles, history, and biology. And during the fishing season, he sells his Mille Lacs Long-Line Walleye Spinner in area tackle shops.

Fellegy still lets loose on those making a buck on fishing, from tournament "jocks" to "seminarians" ("I call them that because they give seminars"), but acknowledges the irony that he himself is getting in on the action. If you can't beat them, join them, he says. In fact, he has fished side-by-side with pro anglers Weaver and Hanson to get a closer look at tournament angling.

"Now I'm busier than I've ever been," he says. "I'm trying to figure out how to survive on land."

And the competitive spirit certainly hasn't died. A week after I fished with Fellegy, I received a letter from him. "That evening I had a couple visitors," he wrote. "One was [the guy] in the Larson boat with his wife. . . . For starters he said, 'Joe, you and that tall guy did a number on us! We haven't had anyone stick it to us like that all summer! Every time we turned around you guys were standing up' They got blanked that day. Also, the launch driver came over and asked me who 'that guy with the funny hat' was. . . . They had six walleyes for the crew. And I found out that [a local guide] had a small-boat guide trip with two guys that morning and scraped up six. You were definitely at the top of the heap that day."

## PICKING YOUR MINNOWS

"The guy who in July or August goes into a bait shop and indiscriminately orders 'a dozen fatheads' will usually catch few if any walleyes using them on Mille Lacs," says Joe Fellegy. Picking the right minnow can boost your catch twentyfold over the angler who chooses the wrong kind, he says.

Minnow size can be critical when fishing the mud flats, especially in late summer. Then Fellegy chooses minnows on the small side, about two inches long, barely larger than what most people would use for crappies. Among his favorites are rainbows (northern redbelly dace), leatherbacks (pearl dace) and fatheads.

When buying fatheads during the summer, reject the large, dark males with spawning tubercles on their snouts. For reasons only walleyes understand, the smaller, lighter-colored females catch more fish. Fellegy goes an extra step by keeping his bait in a white bucket. The fish will try to blend in with their surroundings and grow lighter still.

During cold-water periods, male and female fatheads look alike to fishermen and fish. Then, says Fellegy, "you just take them as they come."

# Chapter Seven

—◆—

# RED RIVER CATFISH:
## An International Resource

Think a moment. Think of northern Minnesota and Canada.

What do you imagine? Birch and spruce forest stretching as far as you can see? Sparkling blue lakes sitting in basins of solid granite? Walleyes swimming in water so clear you can see bottom 10 feet down? Northern pike smashing a bucktail in a bay rimmed with wild rice?

Well, think again. Think of hundreds of square miles of prairie and farmland stretching out toward Saskatoon. Picture a lazy brown river, as thick as gravy, winding back on itself again and again like the bow on a Christmas present. And imagine catfish—catfish that weigh 20 pounds.

Think, too, of how you might levitate a fully equipped bass boat over a shoreline of gumbo two feet deep that won't let you back a trailer to within six feet of water. That's exactly the predicament Henry Drewes and I face as we prepare to launch his boat on the Red River just west of Hallock, 15 miles south of the Manitoba border.

The trip has not begun auspiciously, least of all for Drewes, a fisheries manager for the Minnesota Department of Natural Resources. Drewes feels passionately about protecting the Red River's trophy channel cats, which he calls a "national resource." He worked himself into such a lather discussing it that by the time we reached Karlstad, the jumbo stop signs and flashing red lights marking the town's only significant intersection had become all but invisible to Drewes—like pesky gnats that he brushed aside as he drove straight through toward Manitoba. Within moments he saw flashing red lights of a different sort. I couldn't hear the conversation that followed in the privacy of the state trooper's car, but I imagine it

*Henry Drewes: Passionate protector of Red River catfish.*

contained a lot of yes-sirs and self-deprecating remarks about Drewes' ability to talk and drive at the same time.

But as Drewes chatted, I had a chance to lean back against the hood of his battered Mazda pickup truck and look out over the Red River landscape. It is flat here, flat even to the eyes of a native Minnesotan. It's as flat as water. In fact, it's easy to imagine yourself on a sea of grass, ripe heads of grain rippling like waves in the incessant wind. A thin rim of trees rings the horizon like the shoreline of a huge lake. This land was once the bed of Glacial Lake Agassiz, a sprawling, shallow freshwater sea of the Ice Age that stretched from Big Stone County (the bump on Minnesota's western border) westward nearly the breadth of Saskatchewan and northward nearly to Hudson Bay. Lake Winnipeg and Lake of the Woods are tiny remnants—the puddles remaining after the main body of the lake drained away. Lake Agassiz left a legacy of stunning flatness and a deposit of sediment—the fertile, black Red River Valley soil.

Drewes wrapped up his business, and we drove on to Hallock to get a motel room and then to the river, an abrupt ditch in the otherwise flat landscape. The banks drop precipitously to the water. However much farmers may appreciate the black soil, it sure raises hell with access ramps. The river has fallen several feet during the summer, dumping a thick black quagmire at the end of the concrete ramp. Drewes backs down the steep ramp as far as he dares. "There's no avoiding getting muddy," he says. "The first stop after a Red River fishing trip is always a high-pressure car wash." This from a man who just a couple hours before assured me that "fishing is not supposed to be a lot of work until you get a fish on." We pull on waders and begin wrestling with the bass boat. Sliding it down the bunks, which bend and crack under the weight, we cantilever the boat over the gumbo to the brownish gray river. It plows in steeply, and water pours over the transom. We finally skid the bow over the mud and manage to get Drewes' pickup and trailer back up the steep ramp. How to get the boat *back* onto the trailer is something we can worry about later.

It's about five in the afternoon. The late-summer sun barely touches the river, which is a slurry of mud and fine sediment, billowing in the water as if it were smoke. The steep banks and fringe of trees along the water screen out all evidence of the sea of farmland beyond. Drewes starts the motor and heads slowly upstream. We see a beaver waddling along the muddy bank from a burrow in the riverbank to the succulent willows nearby. Farther up, clam shells show where a raccoon ate. Deer tracks mark the bank. As we reach a steep eroded bank, fingers of tree roots dangle down, at least 15 feet above our heads, reminding us of the savage erosive power of this river when it leaves its banks and floods thousands of square miles of surrounding farmland.

As we move upstream, Drewes scans his depthfinder to find our fishing spot. The Red is essentially a winding trough, 100 feet wide, with an undulating bottom of clay. The familiar pattern of a riffle dropping into a deep pool, which would signal most catfish anglers to drop anchor and start fishing, doesn't hold on this stretch of the Red. Practically none of the riverbed is rocky enough to form a riffle. Logjams, the cover of choice in most catfish streams, have been blown out of the river by the periodic floods. So Drewes looks for spots where the bottom simply drops into a deeper hole.

As we approach the downstream end of a bend, Drewes announces that the river is getting deeper. We continue upstream 100 feet or more until the river begins to shallow up again. Then he spins the boat sideways to the current and we drop anchors at both the bow and stern to hold us broadside to the current. As I set the bow anchor down, the bottom feels like hard clay.

"What's down beneath us?" I ask.

"Eight feet right up here," Drewes says, nodding toward the upstream side of the boat. "And right here," he says, nodding to the downstream side, "it's about twelve feet." Without the depthfinder, I'd have no way of knowing that. My river-reading skills are nearly useless on this stream. The surface is equally placid and uninformative upstream and down.

Drewes pulls out his tackle, a medium-heavy bait-casting rod and a reel spooled with 20-pound test monofilament—the same outfit he'd use for fishing bass in slop or casting spinnerbaits and small bucktails for pike. He threads his line through an egg sinker of about an ounce and ties on a large barrel swivel. To the other end of the swivel he ties a two-and-a-half-foot length of heavy mono and to that, a 4/0 bait hook.

He pops open the cooler and lifts out a fresh 10-inch tullibee (also called a cisco), which he cuts crosswise into pieces one-and-a-half to two inches wide. "The key to catching larger fish is fresh cutbait," he says. He drives his hook through a piece, about 3/4 inch below the back—far enough to hold the bait securely but little enough that the gape of the hook is open and the hook point well exposed.

"That's the popular conception—they're just catfish, they eat anything," he says. "Well, they don't. All the old axioms about a catfish wanting stinkbait is really more folklore than reality. The catfish get to be the size they do by being fish-eaters. They don't grow to 25 pounds by feeding on detritus. If there's a supply of high-oil, high-protein fish available, they won't be grubbing chicken livers or stinkbaits on the bottom."

After I rig my tackle, he takes my hook and sticks it into the head of the tullibee.

"Canadians told me it's always an honor for a guy to get the head off the fish."

"Maybe an honor, but is it effective?"

"Oh, yeah, " he says. "It's a very small mouthful for these catfish."

We lob the bait 50 feet downstream. The egg sinkers plummet to the bottom and roll gently toward the center of the channel. We turn the handles to take the reels out of freespool and take in slack.

"You generally find a pool behind a bend like this," Drewes says. "The current will carry the scent from your bait down throughout the whole pool. The fish will key in on it. That's why you don't spend a lot of time in any one spot, because they would have been there if they were hungry."

With our rods poised and lines taut, we wait. But not for long. Drewes says he feels a tug on his bait. "You'd think a fish that weighs 25 pounds would just pick it up and go, but oftentimes it feels like a little bullhead tapping on it."

After a couple more taps, the fish seems to take the bait, so Drew lowers his rod tip and straightens his arm to give the fish line. As the line tightens, Drewes rears back hard. "I missed him," he says, reeling back a bare hook. Other fish often tap at cutbait, he explains, threading on another piece of tullibee. Carp, suckers of various kinds, sheepshead, carpsuckers—but only channel catfish have mouths big enough to clean the hook.

He flings his baited hook back downstream. This time, however, there are no takers. After a few minutes, we reel in, check our bait, and cast to a different part of the pool. Still nothing. So after a few minutes more, we lift anchor, putter upstream to a new hole, drop anchor, and cast out our baits. Within minutes Drewes feels more tapping. Once again he rears back.

This time he sets the hook into something solid. The fish takes off downstream. Then it settles into a bulldog fight, making several short powerful runs—nothing fast or flashy, but with the power of a train. Soon the fish breaks water in front of me, and I can barely believe my eyes.

"They really do weigh 20 pounds, don't they?" Its mouth alone would accommodate both my fists side by side. It rolls on the surface and dives, disappearing into the murk and stripping line from the reel.

"He isn't ready yet," Drewes says.

"I want to see him leap," I say.

"He just did." Drewes laughs. "That was a tailwalk." Finally he draws the catfish alongside the boat and hands me the rod. The spines of a cat-fish this size are like wooden dowels, too blunt to puncture or cut. So Drewes reaches down and lifts the big cat by the pectoral spines as though they were the handles of a trophy cup. He tapes it at 34 inches and guesses it weighs 18 pounds.

Just a bit on the small side for the Red River.

◄ ◄ ◄

Channel catfish swim in streams large and small throughout Minnesota, including such unlikely northern streams as the Cloquet and St. Louis. As youngsters, they are sleek and silvery gray, punctuated with the black dots that give rise to their Latin name, *Ictalurus punctatus*. As they grow larger, they lose their spots and sleek shapes. Males in particular bulk up until they resemble giant tadpoles with whiskers.

Channel cats belong to the same genus as the common black, brown, and yellow bullheads, which are better suited to lakes and slow-moving streams than the often swift rivers the channel cat prefers. The channel is distantly related to the flathead catfish (*Pylodictis olivaris*), which occupies the deep, log-strewn pools of the lower Mississippi, St. Croix, and Minnesota rivers. (Interestingly, no flatheads swim in the Red River.

## PICKING A RIG FOR CATFISH

The tackle Henry Drewes uses for Red River channel cats, a medium-heavy bait-casting outfit spooled with 20-pound test mono, is more than you'll need for most Minnesota catfishing.

If you're fishing for smaller cats in water without much downed timber or other obstructions, use a lighter spinning or bait-casting outfit with line as light as eight-pound test and a number two bait hook. Cut your bait fish into smaller pieces. In light current , a 1/4-ounce sinker will keep your bait on the bottom.

Conversely, if you're hunting big channel cats or flatheads in log-jams and other woody debris (which the Red River generally lacks) use a muskie-weight bait-casting outfit with 30-pound test line.

When fishing deep turbulent pools, such as those found below dams, you may need two ounces of lead or more to keep your bait down.

Reported flatheads, or "mudcats," as they're commonly called, were probably spawning male channel cats, with swollen, distorted heads and lips, says Drewes.)

Channel cats have taken a rap as garbage eaters, with the implication that they occupy waters too turbid and foul for "real" gamefish. In fact, they often swim side-by-side with walleyes, smallmouth bass, northern pike and, in some streams, muskies. In fact, their diets resemble those of other gamefish. When young, they eat aquatic insects and other small invertebrates, though their diets include some algae and drifting plant material. As they grow larger, they eat more fish, though they continue to take other morsels, living and dead, a habit responsible for the multitude of strange and downright repulsive baits used for catfish over the years, such as bloodbaits and rotting chicken entrails. The practice isn't limited to this country. A Russian angler once told me he fished for giant catfish on the Volga River using a whole duck dressed on a shark hook.

Occasionally baits need no smell or taste at all. Catfish of all kinds occasionally hit artificials. I've caught bullheads on dry flies. A friend recently landed a 30-pound flathead on a light spinning outfit while flipping a small crankbait for smallmouth bass. But channels are more likely than other catfish to strike an artificial. If you fish in a good concentration of channel cats in relatively clear water where they can feed by sight, you stand to catch a few on jigs, crankbaits, spinners, and even weighted flies.

Yet these are exhibition methods: no bread-and-butter cat man would forsake real bait, because catfish are adapted to finding food in dark and turbid conditions when visibility is nil. Sensitive taste buds pepper their entire bodies and are particularly numerous on their whiskerlike barbels.

Catfish are suited to water that is warm as well as turbid. The optimum spawning temperature for channel cats occurs in late June or July, when the water reaches 80 degrees—warm enough to kill a trout. The male builds a nest in an undercut bank amid a clump of roots or downed timber. Their preference for these identifiable lies makes possible the brave southern art of "noodling"—wading along a river, reaching blindly into a crevice and pulling out a catfish of unknown size by the lip, despite the possible presence of snakes and snapping turtles. Once spawning is complete and the fry hatch out, they are protected from other fish by the turbidity to which the catfish is so well adapted.

Channel cats are found from the west slope of the Appalachians, south through Florida and the Gulf Coast well into Mexico. They range through the Missouri River drainage and have been stocked many places out West.

The Red River of the North and Lake Winnipeg are the northernmost extent of its range. The cold climate and peculiarities of the stream itself make the Red River population unique and valuable, Drewes says.

Drewes is in a good position to know. Growing up in Virginia, he learned to catch channel cats on rod and reel, jugs and trotlines, though even he drew the line at noodling. "When I was down in Oklahoma, some of the hill folk down there tried to talk me into going noodling with them, but I figured hell, no, I'm not going to stick my arm up under a bank in the middle of the night."

In 1988, as a fisheries manager with the DNR, Drewes became involved in a study of the river and its catfish after anglers and fish managers voiced concerns that fish might be getting smaller and less numerous because of overfishing.

The first step, Drewes says, was to "clean up" a mishmash of wildly inconsistent regulations by Minnesota, North Dakota, and Manitoba. At the same time, limits became more restrictive. For example, to protect the larger fish in the population, Minnesota and North Dakota allow a daily limit of five channel cats, of which only one can exceed 24 inches (about six pounds).

Next, says Drewes, fish managers needed to learn more about the Red River's catfish and the people who fished for them. In 1990, Minnesota and North Dakota, with help from Manitoba, launched a widescale population assessment, using stationary nets and trotlines to sample catfish from the river's beginning at Breckenridge to the Canadian border. Drewes delighted in getting paid to exercise his childhood skills of setting trotlines—long main lines with dozens of baited hooks dangling below. One end is tied to shore; the other is run at an angle downstream far out into the river and anchored. Over the course of two years, researchers caught, measured and released about 20,000 catfish.

The study confirmed that Red River channel cats live long and grow large, especially in the northern reaches of the river, where they gorge on abundant goldeye and mooneye—silvery fish up to a foot long with the appearance of baby tarpon. "The reason you see 20-pound catfish in the Red River is that substantial forage base," says Drewes. If Drewes is spending several days on the river, he uses small jigs and spinners to catch goldeye and mooneye, which he chops into cutbait. (In clearer water, these species rise readily to dry flies in the evening.) But when time is short, he substitutes tullibees. The survey also provided researchers with important information to use in assessing the effect of fishing pressure on the Red

River catfish (see sidebar on pages 106-107).

Catfishing on the Red River begins in late May and early June, as water temperatures reach the upper 50s. During this early period fishing can be fast. Unfortunately, high water makes boat handling difficult. For that reason, Drewes plans his catfishing trips for the middle of summer. Fishing continues through September and even later, until the water temperature falls into the mid-50s and the fish go off their feed.

●< ●< ●<

Though it's only August, already the fish seem to be slipping into their fall torpor. Drewes' big cat provides the last action of the evening. By nightfall, the air is downright chilly. Rather than wrestle the boat through the mud in the dark, we decide to pull it up on a bank and come back for it in the morning.

When we return, we spot two vehicles that had been parked at the access the night before. One is a car with Missouri plates; the other a pickup and camper from Iowa parked up underneath the highway bridge over the river. The Missourians, a husband and wife, are rigging up tackle as Drewes parks his truck. The man says that catfish up to 25 pounds have kept them coming to the Red River for 20 years. The last couple of days, however, have been poor, he says.

We climb into waders still covered with greasy, gray mud from yesterday. Drewes heads upstream through a thicket of willows to find the boat. Soon I notice activity in the pickup truck. The three occupants begin carrying gear down to a small Lund pulled up on the river bank. One man, stuffed into a pair of extra-large bib overalls, ambles over. His hair's cropped as close as a three-day-old beard. An entire watershed of broken capillaries spread across his baby-smooth cheeks. He and his friends come here about every year, he says. His biggest cat weighed 26 pounds; he's seen them nearly to 30. But the last two days, he says, have been mighty slow.

Drewes' bass boat rounds the bend and comes ashore. I load the gear, hop aboard, and relay the unfortunate news. We begin fishing through the holes we fished the evening before and then continue upriver, spending no more than 20 minutes at a spot in our search for an active fish.

We surmise that the cold front that swept through the area during the past day has put down the catfish, just as sudden cold seems to turn off every other kind of fishing. It's hard to believe that catfish lying beneath 10 feet of opaque brown water could have any awareness of sudden changes in the atmosphere. Drewes has talked to search and rescue divers working the Red who say the river is pitch black just a couple feet down. Yet unquestionably, the fish are in a sulk today. According to Drewes, they are probably lying in the deepest holes and moving very little. Like so much about angling, it is impossible to know why. Our only strategy is to keep moving. "Days like today you have to be at the right place at the right time to find individual fish that are active," Drewes says.

Finally we find some activity. Drewes and I both feel taps on our baits. Drewes drops his rod tip, leans forward and then rips the rod back through the air.

"Here," he says. "You take it."

"No, no. It's your fish."

"Take it. I want you to feel this."

I grab the rod. The fish runs and strips line with the determination of a Malamute on a leash. Each time I bring it toward the surface, it rolls and dives, as if to escape the startling sunlight. Finally, it's played out. I hand Drewes the rod, lean over the boat, grab the pectoral spines, one in each hand, and hoist my trophy aboard. About 16 pounds, Drewes says.

I back the hook out of its rubbery lip and ease it back into the river. It rights itself and disappears into its world of perpetual night.

Our only remaining task now is to winch a 500-pound bass boat across 10 feet of mud and wrestle it onto a trailer.

◄ ◄ ◄

# RED RIVER CATFISH FACTS

The cooperative research project on Red River catfish conducted in 1990–91 by Minnesota and North Dakota, with assistance from Manitoba, has yielded a mother lode of fascinating information and confirmed some earlier research. Among the findings:

• Red River channel catfish are big. Interestingly, and not unexpectedly, fish averaged larger the farther downstream the lines and nets were set. "You're hard-pressed to catch a five-pound catfish in Manitoba," says Drewes. He caught his biggest, a 39-incher that weighed about 28 pounds, near Lockport, Manitoba. An earlier Manitoba creel census showed the channel catfish caught by anglers in Canada averaged 19 pounds.

Why are fish bigger downstream? Perhaps because fishing pressure is greater on the upper river, with its many towns. But mainly the lower river is better suited to growing big fish. The key lies in the forage, the abundant goldeye and mooneye that fill the stomachs of catfish larger than 18 inches. Both these forage species, which eat smaller baitfish and insects, thrive in the wide, slow section of stream near the Canadian border but aren't as abundant in the upper reaches.

Despite the importance of goldeye and mooneye, Red River cats are eclectic in their feeding. Many catfish stomachs contained clam meat (though researchers could not figure out what became of the shells). Drewes tells of one big catfish caught during the Grand Forks catfish derby and displayed in a horse trough. As amazed bystanders looked on, it belched up a squirrel.

• Red River channel catfish grow slowly and live long. Channel cats can't put on weight until the water temperature reaches 70 degrees. As a result, they may grow only half as fast as fish in the southern United States, where the growing season is longer.

Red River cats may grow slowly, but they live for a long time. Researchers found Red River fish up to 26 years old—twice the age of fish in the South. In the Red, 20-year-old fish will weigh about 20 pounds.

- Red River cats, contrary to their sluggish appearance, are international travelers. One fish tagged near Drayton was netted by a commercial walleye fisherman in Lake Winnipeg 200 miles away by water. Another fish, tagged by Canadians near the border, turned up 14 days later near Hecla Island in Lake Winnipeg, 250 miles downstream.

Drewes says Minnesota and North Dakota hope to follow the population survey with additional research about angling pressure and its economic contributions. The states would also like to tag catfish with radio transmitters to learn more about the habitat the fish require. Manitoba has already conducted some of this research. These studies provide fish managers with the baseline data they need to determine if sport fishing or other influences, such as pollution, are harming the catfish population. So far, Red River cats are faring well, Drewes says, but two threats loom large.

First is the increasing popularity of the Red River cats. "This population is unique," says Drewes. "It's sensitive to over-fishing if people don't practice catch and release."

The second threat comes in the form of dozens of flood-control projects scheduled for Red River tributaries. If they do their job too well or regulate flows in unnatural ways, they could prevent catfish and other fish from swimming over or around dams during upstream spawning runs each spring. "We're screwing around with the whole water flow cycle on the river because of all these little pork barrels on the tributaries," Drews says.

# Chapter Eight

— ⊷ —

# UPTOWN BASS:
## A Big-Fish Spot

Chet Meyers is lost in a reverie, adrift in a fisherman's dream world. He has just caught the largemouth of a lifetime. Not only is it the biggest bass he ever caught; he has caught it on a beautiful day in late summer under a mackerel sky and a dead, dead calm on the water and not a boat—not a single soul—on the lake, even though we are surrounded at the moment by two million people.

We are on Lake Calhoun, sandwiched between wealthy Kenwood homes and the high-energy, artsy Uptown area of Minneapolis, where the clothes are black and the earrings are in your nose.

And the bass weighs nearly seven pounds.

"Oh, thank you Great Spirit," he says.

Dressed this morning in red flannel shirt and olive canvas brimmed hat, Meyers is a professor of humanities who teaches philosophy at Metropolitan State University in Minneapolis. He also teaches a class on fishing and writes how-to stories for outdoor magazines. Since he has lived in Minneapolis, he has become a guru of metro lakes and the tremendous bass fishing they provide.

When he came to town in 1968, his first purchase was a canoe for duck hunting. Before long, he began fishing the chain of lakes—Brownie, Cedar, Isles, and Calhoun—right outside his door. "I found an incredible fishery that no one was taking advantage of," he says. "When I came in with stories of all these fish I caught—I nearly always let them go—no one would believe me. Okay, I said, I don't care. I figured I had them all to myself."

*Chet Meyers: Guru of bass fishing*
*on the metro lakes.*

Indeed, he often did, with the exception of a few bank anglers, sail-boaters and, more recently, sail boarders. None were much of a threat to the fishing. The bank anglers couldn't reach many good spots, especially after the weeds came up, completely hemming in the shoreline by early summer. (Shore fishing has become even more difficult in recent years as Eurasian watermilfoil has completely blockaded the shallows.) Of course, the sailors were far more interested in what was above the water than what lay below. "In all these years, I've met two people—two people—who fish these lakes seriously," says Meyers.

Yet the lakes can offer up rich rewards. On one occasion Meyers's neighbor caught bass of over four pounds, five pounds, and six pounds on nearly consecutive casts. Meyers scouted out a point in Lake of the Isles where he could catch fish trip after trip. And because of the relatively light fishing pressure, each year they got bigger. Four of his friends caught the biggest bass of their lives from the spot. Finally, Meyers wrote a story he called "The Class of '75" about the super class of bass that year. He continued to enjoy unbelievable fishing until well into the next decade, when the bass began disappearing through inevitable angler harvest and sheer old age. "They treated us well, those fish," he says. "My wife thought I abused them."

That was before Eurasian watermilfoil appeared. During the last several years, this gangly plant, an Old World alien that began infesting Minnesota waters in 1987, began spreading across the shallow areas of Minneapolis lakes in dense mats that blocked off boat and canoe travel and crowded out native plants such as cabbage, a magnet to most kinds of game fish. "We used to have wonderful cabbage, but it's all gone," Meyers says. "Milfoil screwed it all up."

Bass appeared unharmed by this sudden abundance of cover, but the weeds rendered normal fishing methods nearly useless during the height of summer. The impenetrable beds of milfoil force anglers like Meyers to dunk jigs or bait into the openings in the weeds—a method Meyers finds tedious—or concentrate their efforts along the outer weedlines. "Milfoil reduced you to edge fishing, which is kind of boring," he says. "I like to be able to troll and to throw up on flats and points and work something across the flat and then skip it down the drop." The only small consolation from the milfoil invasion is that an angler without a depthfinder can find the major breaklines in city lakes by following the edges of the milfoil beds. "You can see exactly what the bottom looks like," says Meyers.

Milfoil or not, the methods Meyers uses to catch big bass on Minneapolis lakes will produce results anywhere in the state. The only special adaptation Meyers has made is his choice of fishing boats, since both Minneapolis and St. Paul ban the use of gasoline outboards on their lakes, a restriction Meyers doesn't resent in the least because it preserves an island of peace and quiet in a sea of noise and bustle. "I think it's reduced the fishing pressure, too," says Meyers, "because most people aren't willing to fish from a canoe or to plop a bass boat down and move around simply on the electric motor."

This morning Meyers is loading up his canoe, which is perched on a dolly in the driveway of his Kenwood home. The canoe—a short, wide aluminum model—is tricked out with comfortable nylon-web seats with folding wood-slat backrests. A wooden bracket mounted across the stern holds an electric trolling motor. A flasher rests just forward of the rear seat. Today, because two of us will fish, Meyers has stowed the battery under the rear seat. When he is alone, it rests up in the bow to counterbalance his own weight. I toss my bait-casting rod in with his own assortment of spinning and bait-casting rigs, and we're off.

"Off" in this case is down to Lake of the Isles at the end of the block. Meyers lifts the bow of the canoe and pulls it rickshaw-style down the street. Foot traffic around the lake is just beginning to build. Senior citizens in walking shoes and windbreakers march along as though off to war. Young men and women in neon shorts Rollerblade along the asphalt paths and speed along on bicycles. One fellow is walking a Shar-Pei, the most wrinkled dog in existence—a small boxer in a Great Dane's hide. The dog is frightened by our canoe and has to be coaxed around it.

Meyers raises the bow while I pull out the dolly, a compact arrangement of two-by-fours on a child's wagon axle and wheels. Meyers sets the canoe in the water and stashes the dolly amidships. We climb aboard and push off. "Canoe, how are you? *Who* are you?" Meyers wonders aloud. A recent book, which he finished just the day before, has kept him off the water nearly all summer.

Once out in the bay, Meyers stops paddling. The canoe drifts silently. He pulls out a bag of tobacco. "People think I'm on drugs, but I perform a simple tobacco ceremony before I start fishing." He takes a pinch of tobacco, as though it were snuff. He smells it, holds it momentarily above the lake, spreads it on the water, and mixes it into the water with a swirl of the paddle as he pivots the canoe a quarter turn. Six times he does this, once for each of the four winds and once each for the Great Spirit and Mother Earth.

"Where did you learn it?" I ask.

"Black Elk, a Lakota medicine man," he answers. More specifically,

111

from the book *Black Elk Speaks*. "I was looking for more spirituality in nature. Christianity has always seemed so hostile to nature."

Off we paddle with hostility toward no one, except perhaps the rafts of ducks swimming in the shallow bay. The heads of the young drake mallards are just beginning to turn green. "I look at them all year, and they look like nice little birds," Meyers observes. "In fall, they begin to look like food."

In spring, before they become choked with milfoil, these shallow bays of Lake of the Isles provide Meyers some of his most frantic largemouth fishing. The bays warm more quickly than deeper, windswept lakes such as Calhoun. Bass pour into these shallows, especially those with firm, sandy bottoms, to spawn. Spawning occurs when the water temperature is in the mid-60s, usually in early May. Many years, if summer is slow in coming, the bass will remain in these areas until well after the season opens. "I remember coming down there with my neighbor and catching 26 bass in an hour and they were all between two and five pounds," Meyers says. Typically at that time of year he pitches small (number two) in-line silver-bladed spinners or black and silver floating Rapalas toward shore and retrieves them slowly. The treble hooks on these lures, however, snag every obstruction in their path, so once the weeds come up, Meyers switches to his all-time favorite bass lure, the plastic worm.

Unfortunately, some of his best early summer spots have been ruined by the spreading cancer of milfoil—in particular, a sandy point, once flanked by cabbage beds, that led into a 10-foot-deep hole. "This used to be my secret spot, but now I tell people because it's no good anymore," he says with disgust. The fact that this particular summer has been cold enough to retard milfoil growth is small consolation. "This used to be such a good bass-fishing lake," Meyers says. "It makes me sick to think about it."

As spring turns to summer, many bass migrate to deeper water. Action turns from shallow cover and the inside edges of weedbeds to the outside edges of deep weedbeds and midlake humps and reefs. Because it's late August, we stow the paddles, and Meyers switches on the trolling motor to speed us through the shallows of Lake of the Isles. No one would use this rig in a bass tournament, but it does move along smoothly at fast walking speed. Soon we reach the end of Isles, scoot under an overpass marked with graffiti and emerge at Lake Calhoun. Already it is nearly 8 A.M., yet the only boats on the water are a cluster of unmanned sailboats moored at the north end of the lake. It's damn peaceful here—more so than at a lake in resort country where motors are allowed.

Calhoun, Meyers tells me, is a deep-water haven, contrary to

## SEEING UNDERWATER

One of the keys to successfully fishing a deep-water point or hump for bass and other species is accurately visualizing the contours of the lake bottom, even though it lies out of sight.

Once you find a hump or other structure with your depthfinder, move slowly back and forth across the top of it to gain an understanding of its dimensions and how sharply it drops from shallow water to deep. Then drop marker buoys at important points along the structure to provide reference points.

By accurately picturing underwater structure, you'll know whether you catch fish on the "flat" (the top of the structure), on the break (the steep slope into deeper water) or at the base, where the break ends and deep water begins. Then you can concentrate your efforts in those areas and easily find them on your next visit.

appearances. "It looks like a soup bowl, but boy, it's anything but a soup bowl. It's incredible. It's got one of the most convoluted bottoms."

We begin working one of Meyers' favorites spots, a deep, complex hump that rises from more than 20 feet of water to less than six feet deep. Down the middle runs a slot 15 feet deep. All around, the structure reaches out in a number of smaller bars. "It's just like a glove with all sorts of fingers and indentations," Meyers says.

He turns on his depthfinder, a simple flasher, and begins circling the hump. "Guy in my fishing class got a liquid-crystal depthfinder," he remarks as he maneuvers the canoe. "And I warned him, 'You're going to see fish and you're going to sit on them all day.' Sure enough, that's what happened. He said, 'God, they were huge!' 'Did you ever wonder what they were,' I asked him. 'They were carp!' Big carp in this lake. Boy, it's scary. Twenty pounds. Follow your canoe and wait for you to fall overboard. I've been thinking of opening a bed and breakfast and inviting people from England. It's just phenomenal."

When he's satisfied that he has found the part of the hump he is looking for, he tosses out a marker buoy. Then he backs off and begins to fish around this reference point. "If you don't have marker buoys, if you don't know what you're doing, you can really waste your time on this lake," he says.

While I rip a spinnerbait along the top of the high spots of the hump, Meyers works the breaklines with the inevitable plastic worm. If he were fishing in the midst of slop, he would use a Texas-rigged worm, with the hook point buried in the body of the worm. But since he is working the edges of the weeds, he ties on a bare jig, and threads on a six-inch black worm, leaving the hook point fully exposed. He vacillates between 1/8-ounce and the 1/4-once jigs for his bassing. He likes the lighter jig because the smaller-diameter hook penetrates the tough lip of a bass better; he likes the heavier jig because it sinks faster. Today he opts for the 1/4 ounce.

Meyers uses a medium-weight spinning outfit to fish, though many folks prefer a bait-casting rig. He casts out and watches the line as the worm sinks to the bottom. Then he reels in slack and lifts the worm several feet through a combination of sweeping his rod tip upward and reeling in line. Then he stops reeling and lowers the rod tip to let the worm sink back down to the bottom. All the time, he watches the line. "When I'm fishing with a worm and a jig, I watch the point where the line intersects the water for little twitches to the left or right or for it to stop." When he spots a suspicious twitch, he strikes immediately with a long sweep of the rod. "By the time you feel a fish, it's always too late."

Today, unfortunately, no twitches are forthcoming. I do, however, catch a small tiger muskie on the spinnerbait. Several city lakes have been stocked with this hybrid of the northern pike and muskie. In fact, the state record tiger muskie, a 33-pound, eight-ounce hybrid nearly four feet long, was recently caught in Calhoun. Though these hybrids occur in nature, they are rare. Wild or stocked, they are always infertile, and that is one reason fisheries managers like them. Stocking a large predator such as the tiger muskie always carries the risk that the fish will take to its new environment *too* well, become overabundant, and destroying its forage, to the detriment of other game fish in the ecosystem. The danger is minimized, however, if the stocked predator cannot reproduce. If, for example, the number of tiger muskies gets too great, fish managers simply stock fewer or none at all, without fear that the fish will perpetuate its own numbers. The population will dwindle as fish are caught or die of other causes.

We are after bass today, however, so we motor down the lake to another of Meyers' favorite spots—a deep doglegged bar that, in places, is barely more than a few yards wide. "I wish I had a geologist tell me what it is and why it's here," Meyers says. "It's bizarre. It doesn't make sense." From experience, Meyers has learned the bar is hard and gravelly and has few weeds. As he motors slowly along, he crosses the top of the bar in nine feet of water and tosses out a marker buoy. As he moves off just two canoe lengths, the water drops to 35 feet. Then he turns direction and reacquaints himself with the way the bar runs and bends. "I'm more fascinated by structure than by fish," he confesses. "I fish this piece of structure on the St. Croix up near Taylors Falls—never caught a thing, but it was beautiful. I was just fascinated by it."

When he finds the hook of the dogleg, he tosses out another marker. For awhile, we rake the structure beneath us with plastic worms and crankbaits with no results. "It's one of those days the fish want real meat," Meyers comments, as he puts away one spinning rod and readies another. When I called the previous evening, he said, "I think I've got some desiccated crawlers in the basement." What he found, he says now, rummaging through the tackle under the canoe seat, are nightcrawlers left over from May, three months ago. "Oh, Geez, I've got one crawler," he says as he stirs the bedding with his fingers. "You know what that means. We're dead."

Meyers rigs his crawler on a slip-sinker rig, hooking the crawler in the nose. He flips this out, leaves the bail open, pinches the line between his forefinger and the rod handle, and trolls slowly along the top of the bar. "Why can't I remember the names of the people my wife introduces me to, but I remember every spot in the world I've caught a fish?" he muses. "This is a big-fish spot. The only fish I've caught here have been big fish. Al Lindner first introduced me to the concept of big-fish spots. Until then, I had just thought that wherever you caught fish you caught fish."

Within seconds, Meyers says he feels a tap. He lets a couple feet of line peel off, turns the reel handle to flip the bail, takes in slack, and rears back on the rod.

Nothing.

He reels in, checks the worm, and sends it back to work. Again he feels a tug, again he sets the hook. Again he gets nothing.

"Bluegills," he mutters.

Each time he checks his worm, it is shorter and shorter. Finally, he rears back into a fish. The reel sizzles.

"This thing's got shoulders."

"It's probably a really big carp, Chet."

"Doggone, that's what I'm starting to think. Wait. It's a bass, it's a bass."

Meyers grabs his short-handled landing net and slips it under a big largemouth that moments later pulls his scale down to four pounds even. "Great Spirit, that was a treat," he says as he lets the fish go.

By now, Meyers' crawler is gone entirely. But poking through his gear, he finds another plastic bait carton, this one with four or five withered specimens. He rigs up, tosses the bait overboard, and within moments hooks another fish. "This is not as big," he announces nonchalantly. "Geez!" he says, as the fish scoots around the stern of the canoe and peels off line. Then it rises to the surface and keeps right on going, clearing the water by several inches as it shakes its head, spraying water in every direction before falling heavily into the lake, and Meyers finally realizes what it is he has on the end of his line.

"God, that's a hog! It's huge, it's huge, it's just huge."

Fool that he is, he asks me to net it as he finally brings it alongside the canoe. I decide not to tell him the number of fish I have set free with a landing net over the years. As I lower the net, the bass darts suddenly to the side, just past the hoop. Luckily, the hook misses the net mesh. Meyers regains control and leads the fish to the net a second time. This time I scoop it up, and only then do I realize how large this bass is. Had I known earlier, I would have made him net it himself.

"It's the biggest bass I ever caught in my life," he says breathlessly. He lays it across the thwart of the canoe and tapes it—only 23 inches but it looks like it has swallowed a football. It pulls Meyers' hand-held scale to just a shade under seven pounds.

"People ask, 'Why do you want to fish the city lakes when you can go to Brainerd?'" Meyers says as he slips his trophy back into the water. "I say, 'Aw, I don't know. Just lazy.'"

◄ ◄ ◄

## HOW TO MAKE A SLIP-SINKER RIG

String a 1/8-ounce walking sinker onto your line. Then pinch on a small split shot (B or BB) onto the line about two feet above the end. Tie on a number six short-shanked bait hook, using a snell or clinch knot. Hook the worm once through the nose. Fish the bait with your spinning reel bail open or your bait-casting reel in freespool.

A slip-sinker catches bass and other species so effectively partly because it lets the fish take the bait without resistance from the sinker or your reel. And for that very reason, fish often suck down the bait and are hooked mortally in the throat.

Reduce this problem by reacting within just a few seconds to a bite. If a fish you want to release is hooked deeply, leave the hook and cut the line rather than rip out the hook.

Better yet, if you intend to release your fish, fish bait on a jig or stick entirely to artificial lures.

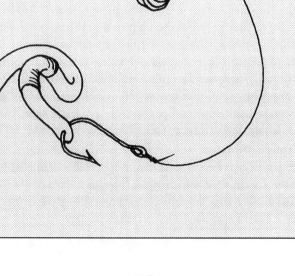

# TWIN CITIES TROPHIES

More than one of my friends, when told of big bass in Twin Cities lakes, have remarked, "Oh, they stock those lakes?" as though somehow bass have forgotten how to spawn. Really, the prospect of trophy largemouths in city lakes shouldn't surprise anyone because these waters have the two key ingredients to produce large fish: good habitat and a lack of real fishing pressure.

To flourish, largemouth bass need the following habitat, which city lakes generally have in abundance:

• Spawning areas of shallow water with a firm bottom of sand or sand and mud.

• Cover, such as beds of rooted aquatic plants like cabbage, to provide hiding places for young bass and ambush points for adults.

• Abundant forage, which to a largemouth can be almost anything that will fit in its mouth. Sunfish are common prey. So are various species of minnows. Cannibalism is rife among bass.

• Adequate dissolved oxygen, especially during the winter, when ice seals lakes and decaying vegetation consumes dissolved oxygen. The resultant "winterkill" is common in shallow, fertile, weedy lakes, but rare in large, deep lakes, such as Calhoun, Harriet, or Cedar.

"If the habitat is maintained, the fish are going to be there," says Bruce Gilbertson, East Area fisheries supervisor for the Minnesota Department of Natural Resources. Looming problems such as infestation by milfoil and high-nutrient runoff from lawns and streets, which can cause algae blooms and a smothering proliferation of weeds, has not yet hurt fish populations.

But having a lot of fish does not guarantee big fish, says Gilbertson. "In many respects, it's like trees. You're not going to have large trees if you harvest every 50 years." And a lake won't have large fish if they are caught and cooked as soon as they reach a pound, as they are in some heavily fished waters.

But in Minneapolis and St. Paul, big fish are inadvertently protected by a ban on gasoline outboards. Minneapolis further restricts access by requiring all boats or canoes to display city permits. As a result, sophisticated anglers—those armed with bass boats, depthfinders, and the knowledge necessary to use a variety of effective fishing techniques—rarely visit these lakes. What angling pressure exists comes almost entirely from shore anglers. As a result, the deep-water structure that holds large bass throughout much of the year is rarely fished.

Vadnais Lake provides another example of protecting fish by limiting access, says Gilbertson. Ice fishing or the use of boats is prohibited on Vadnais, part of the area's water supply system. Any fishing must be from shore. As a result, the average size of both game fish and sunfish is well above the average in nearby lakes.

On other lakes, pressure is reduced in different ways. For example, on Lake Waconia the DNR has instituted a 18- to 21-inch slot limit, meaning all bass in that range must be released. On Steiger Lake, all game fish, including bass, must be set free.

# Chapter Nine

———————— ⊷ ————————

# BIG BLUEGILLS:
## *Few and Far Between*

With his bushy beard, slicked-up pompadour, and a face as tanned as cowhide, Dick "the Griz" Grzywinski looks more like one of the original Hell's Angels than a fishing guide, more at home on a chopped Harley than at the tiller of a Yamaha 60-horse. Yet here we are aboard his fishing boat, puttering out to an underwater hump on South Lindstrom Lake to fish for, of all things, bluegills.

Among serious anglers, Grzywinski is known as the master of the bizarre technique called "ripping," or as Grzywinski himself sometimes refers to it, simply "the Technique." He trolls quickly along a reef line, casts a jig and minnow out behind, gives it a good rip, lowers it down, and rips it again. The Technique has been so astonishingly successful and hard to duplicate that Grzywinski has become known as a walleye wizard and—to his chagrin—a specialist.

"Everybody's got me pinned down as a walleye guide, you know, but I do it all—walleyes, catfish, sturgeon. I do it all."

Not only will he guide for anything; he'll guide anywhere. "I don't guide on any one lake. I guide on all of them, wherever people want to go." Just recently he hired out to guide on Lake of the Woods for walleyes. "Never been there in my life, but I did better than their guides that have been out there every day."

Sounded to me like the makings of an ulcer.

"Every day is pressure," Grzywinski says. "Guys ask me why I don't fish tournaments. I got one everyday. I got two guys in a boat that, if we don't get fish, I'll never see again."

*Dick Grzywinski: The anytime,*
*anywhere fishing guide, searching for*
*big bluegills on South Lindstrom Lake.*

Just recently, he took a newspaper writer out for muskies on a lake in the heart of the St. Paul suburbs. Within minutes they caught their fish. Before the afternoon was over, they also had several follows. Who was the reporter? I ask. Grzywinski puzzles a moment and then admits he's bad at names. "All I can remember is the bottoms of lakes," he says.

The Griz will also guide anytime. He's one of the area's few ice-fishing guides. Winter fishing with Grzywinski can be a daunting challenge because, as his friends and clients know, he is absolutely tireless while on a bite. In subzero temperatures he can hover endlessly over a hole in the ice, baiting hooks and unhooking fish, without a thought to the weather. His fingers, as thick as dill pickles, seem impervious to cold.

He grew up on St. Paul's east side, fishing metro lakes like Phalen. "I fished that all my life," he says. "Got a 27-pound northern out of Phalen." Ten years ago, frustrated by full-time work at a warehouse, he began guiding. "I knew I was good at it, so I started guiding at Winnibigoshish. I guided at the *In-Fisherman* Camp Fish Jamboree, and I took the best guide award a couple years in a row. Things started getting better and better. More articles. People started calling more and more.

"Did something 33 years of my life I hated, so I just quit and went guiding. Never be a millionaire, but it's something I love to do."

Of all the species of fish Grzywinski hunts for as a guide, few are more difficult to find than big bluegills. The reason: catch-and-release fishing for the popular and tasty panfish has never caught on. No laws require it. Liberal limits of 30 sunfish of any species apply to all state lakes. And while anglers willingly accept that heavy fishing pressure can drive down the average size of northern pike, bass, or walleyes, few seem to have thought that the same might be true of sunfish.

Fisheries managers long believed that "stunting" was responsible for the proliferation of tiny sunnies in many heavily fished lakes. According to the theory, an abundance of good sunfish spawning habitat and an absence of predator fish because of overfishing causes an explosion in the sunfish population. Competition for food intensifies, growth rates plummet, and the lake soon fills with sunfish the size of potato chips.

While stunting does occur, more and more fisheries managers—and panfish anglers—are coming to believe that sunfish, like any other fish, are adversely affected by overfishing. In fact, cropping off the larger fish may in fact increase competition among smaller fish and slow down growth rates. In this scenario, it is the overfishing of large panfish that causes stunting; not stunting that causes the absence of large fish.

Be that as it may, bluegills' popularity has made it tough to find big ones—tough even for someone who fishes as many lakes as Grzywinski does. "Lakes with big panfish are getting few and far between," he says. "Bluegills are in trouble. People are fishing them down to nothing. They get on a good bluegill bite, and they just fish it right out. They keep going back for limit after limit."

As evidence, Grzywinski cites the case of Sunrise Lake near Lindstrom. Surrounded by private land with no public access, Sunrise saw few anglers until one lakeshore owner hit upon the idea of charging ice fishermen for access.

"One winter and one spring they fished the whole lake out," Grzywinski says. "It's pressure. I heard talk they were going there three, four times a day, taking their limit, going home, coming back." Once he counted 87 cars driving onto the ice in a single 15-minute period. "Now you go there and catch 'em, and they're like silver dollars."

## FLY-FISHING FOR BLUEGILLS

Fly-fishing for spawning bluegills is one of angling's visceral pleasures, a thrilling no-brainer. The game is filled with anticipation, action, and the aesthetic satisfaction of feeling these dogged little fighters double over a long, light rod as they rip circles in the water.

Light tackle lets sunfish show off their spunk. I like a four- or five-weight rod—just what you'd use for trout in a small stream. Any floating line will do since short casts are the rule. Use a six- to eight-foot-long leader that tapers to about 5X (about four-pound test).

The most effective flies I have ever used for shallow-lying bluegills are a small popper and nymph rigged in tandem. Tie the popper (about the size of a pencil eraser) directly onto your leader. Then clinch knot a one- to three-foot length of 5X leader material to the bend of the popper hook. Tie a small weighted nymph, such as a number 12 Hare's Ear, to the other end of the mono. Vary the length of the dropper according to the depth of the water.

Then work along the edge of the bluegill's nesting colonies on foot or by boat, dropping the flies into the thick of the sunfish. Work the popper with small pops. The commotion attracts the bluegills, though most fish will snatch the nymph. Many will suck the nymph down deep, but if you pinch down the barb, the fish will be easy to unhook if you use a needle-nose or hemostat.

So the challenge for someone who wants to catch slab-sided sunfish is not the fishing but the finding. Grzywinski looks for sizeable lakes without public boat ramps and tries to wheedle with private landowners for access. Backwoods lakes without decent access roads or boat ramps are also good bets. Grzywinski also searches out lakes that winterkill occasionally. As a wintertime lack of oxygen kills most of the fish in a lake, surviving sunfish get a chance to grow big without intense competition from hordes of their cohorts. Moreover, a reputation for winterkill probably keeps many anglers away.

Once you've found a good lake, the fishing is easy, Grzywinski says.

In spring look for spawning bluegills in shallow bays, where the males scoop out colonies of circular nests on a sand or gravel bottom in water a foot to five feet deep. The fish are concentrated, aggressive, and easy to catch. If they're inclined to hit on top, which they usually are that time of year, Grzywinski tosses out a popper with a fly rod. If they're reluctant to come to the surface, Grzywinski pitches tiny jigs into the nesting areas. Try 1/32- to

## HOW TO TIE A SLIP-BOBBER KNOT

Many anglers buy their bobber stops in tackle stores, but it's a simple matter to make your own. Simply lay a six-inch length of heavy braided line along your monofilament. Form a loop in the braided line. Then wind one of the ends of the braided line a half-dozen times around the mono and the parallel strand of braided line. Pull both ends of braided line to tighten the knot. Clip the ends close to the knot, which you can slide up or down the mono to control the depth of the bobber.

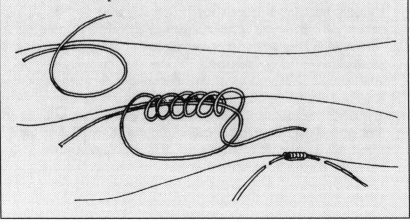

1/64-ounce jigs, depending on the size and aggressiveness of the fish.

Fishing becomes more challenging in midsummer, after the fish complete their spawning and head for deeper water. The little guys are still easy to catch, as any kid fishing along shore can tell you, but the bruisers are tougher to come by. Grzywinski looks for good numbers of these bigger fish in and along deep weed beds. Best of all are deep cabbage-covered bars and humps, where bluegills feed on aquatic insects, other invertebrates, and small fish.

Grzywinski's favorite technique is the one he shows me today—fishing a leech below a slip bobber. South Lindstrom, unfortunately, doesn't fit Grzywinski's criteria as a top spot for big bluegills. It's served by a boat ramp and is fished heavily because of its reputation for large bass and plentiful panfish. Yet it's a productive lake, and Grzywinski is betting that he can locate some bluegills in spots overlooked by most fishermen.

We motor out to a weed-covered hump, which lies a few hundred yards off one shore. He tosses out a marker where the hump tops out at about six feet deep, and then trolls slowly around the marker. "I always look the structure over good before I land down on it so I know what I'm fishing," he says.

Normally in mid-August he looks for big sunnies in 15 to 18 feet of water, but the cool summer has kept water temperatures down. As a result, the bluegills are occupying weeds only six or eight feet deep—a pattern more typical of fall. "Doggone cold summer's got 'em really screwy this year," he says.

Once Grzywinski can visualize the structure beneath us, he tosses out the anchor along one edge of the weed bed. Depending on the conditions and where the fish seem to be located, Grzywinski fishes along the weedline as well as in the thick of the weeds.

Grzywinski uses a spinning outfit with six- or four-pound test line and a long rod to help take up slack and set the hook when the bobber has drifted a long way from the boat.

He first threads a commercial bobber stop on the line to control the depth of the slip bobber. Next he threads on a plastic bead a bit bigger than a BB and, after he pokes around in his tackle box, a suitable slip bobber. If he were fishing just for sunnies, he would choose something small, but today, because he's hoping to pick up some larger game fish, he picks a float the size of a pecan.

Next he ties on a number six long-shanked bait hook. Again, if he were fishing only for sunfish, he might choose an eight. Then he clamps a number four split shot on the line about 10 inches above the hook, and a slightly smaller number five right underneath it. That configuration seems to tangle less than two sinkers of equal size, he says. With a smaller float, he would use smaller split shot.

Grzywinski clamps a small lead "depthfinder" onto his hook and lowers it to the bottom. He pinches the line at the surface and then slides the bobber stop to a point about a foot lower, which means he will be fishing about a foot off the bottom—just where he wants to be when fishing for large bluegills.

Next he reaches into a bucket of medium-sized leeches—not the small ones you might expect. "They're one of the best baits you can use because you can catch anything from crappies to walleyes on them. I don't care what lake you go on, a leech will work anyplace," he says. Grzywinski hooks the leech in the side, down toward the sucker.

"See?" he says, lowering the hooked leech into the water, "here's what happens. He swims like a minnow. That's what you want."

After I rig my line, he nods toward the edge of the weeds. "Just throw your cork over there," he says. "You should get a bite. Bass or walleye, it'll go *boop* out of sight right away. But if it's a sunfish, he'll fool with it awhile." For that reason if he's fishing exclusively for panfish he sometimes uses pieces of leech on a tiny bait hook or jig.

Within minutes fish find our leeches. At first I jump the gun, trying to set the hook too soon, and succeed only in bringing shiny, clean hooks back to the boat. "These sunfish are real tricksters," says Grzywinski. "You got to stay on your toes with those sons of guns on a leech."

Soon, after watching Grzywinski, I get the hang of letting the bobber disappear about two seconds—an agonizingly long time for someone used to fishing artificial flies and lures—and then reeling in slack before ripping the rod to set the hook. We begin catching walleyes, bass and, yes, good-sized bluegills. "They ain't monster sunfish, but for the metro, they're good sunfish," says Grzywinski.

I ask Grzywinski if he sometimes runs into hoards of tiny bluegills in a lake he knows to hold large sunfish.

"The big sunfish are down underneath the little ones," he says. "If the little ones don't get it, the big ones will."

"How do you get beyond the little ones?" I ask.

"Well, you just got to keep donating."

By donating a lot and often, Grzywinski has caught some impressive sunfish, including a two-pound, seven-ounce bluegill he caught in Pelican Lake near Orr.

Pelican was once reputed to be one the state's best lakes for big bluegills, but like many others it has been heavily fished and today offers up few trophies. "I haven't caught a keeper in two years," Grzywinski says.

So the Griz keeps on searching—for good lakes without an access, for little-known lakes that occasionally winterkill, and backcountry water not often visited by the panfishing crowds. And he keeps after state fisheries professionals to provide more protection to panfish as well as other species. "They're doing something," he says, "but they're not doing it fast enough. People have got to return those fish."

<br>

## FINDING THE ELUSIVE CRAPPIE

Crappies, one of Minnesota's most popular panfish, are easy to catch in the spring, when they congregate and spawn in shallow water amid brush or last year's growth of bulrushes. But warming water brings on one of the summer's great mysteries: Where do all the big crappies go?

"They're like a mystery fish," says Dick Grzywinski. "They go out in the deep water and suspend. They sit out in the deep water all over."

Trying to find a roving school of crappies in hundreds of acres of water can be nigh on to impossible. In the past, Grzywinski has trolled a small, unweighted Flatfish over 20 to 25 feet of water, hoping to find crappies. "Boy, would they slam that thing," he says. But those catches are just chance encounters. Hoping to increase his odds, he looks for crappies that are associated with *some* kind of structure. His favorite places are the same deep weed-covered bars that hold big bluegills in the summer. The best spot to try is the very tip of a deep underwater point.

Crappies often suspend, even in weeds. So if Grzywinski's in 15 feet of water, he usually starts fishing about eight to 12 feet deep. If he doesn't get fish, he tries deeper.

Usually he uses a slip-bobber rig, baited with a crappie minnow, small white jig, or jig tipped with a minnow. A favorite lure, especially early in the year, is a jig tipped with a number two Fire Ball Jig-N-Minnow, a small plastic minnow that looks so plain and stiff that Grzywinski couldn't believe it would catch fish until he tried it.

The choice of a slip bobber is important. Grzywinski likes a Tel'Bob, which flips over when a fish strikes. Grzywinski doesn't care that the bobber signals a strike; he just likes the way it rocks in a slight chop, causing the bait below to jiggle. "It's one of those little differences people overlook," he says.

# Chapter Ten

---◄►---

# CANOE COUNTRY SMALLMOUTH:
## Searching High and Low

Come late May and early June, the first long days of spring warm the rocky face of the Boundary Waters Canoe Area Wilderness. The aspen and birch leaves sprout tender, lively green leaves. The portage trails finally dry out and allow easy passage from one lake to another. Bulrushes poke above water in the back bays. And big bass—quite a lot of bass over three pounds—are beginning to move into shallow water to spawn. Anyone can be a smallmouth expert.

The game is simple. We prowl along the shore in a canoe, looking for the right kind of rock. Not just any kind will do. We don't waste much time with weather-beaten rocky slabs that slope into the clear water, unbroken monoliths for as deep as the eye can see. This might hold trout or a big northern pike in summer, but offers little to a bass with love on its mind. Instead, we look where the shoreline tucks into a bay and escapes the meanest winds and wildest waves, where we might find a sloping beach of sand, gravel, baseball-sized cobble, and a few boulders. All the better if a log or two lie on the bottom or a big pine has fallen straight out into the water. Then we pull out our fly rods and gently lay poppers or Dahlberg Divers within a yard of shore. We let them sit, and if nothing happens after a few seconds, pop them gently. Nothing yet? We pop them several times or strip in line so the divers scoot beneath the surface and then float back up to the top. Still nothing? Then we lift up our lines and cast again, a few feet farther down the shoreline. Chances are, within a few minutes, a big smallmouth will pounce on the bug and rip the living hell out of the still surface of the lake, leaping and thrashing until we bring it to the canoe. It is brainless fishing—completely of the moment, visceral, and sensuous.

These are the times John Herrick loves, too. Herrick, a burly, handsome artist-turned-fishing guide, grew up in the Chicago area. He first came to this region as a 12-year-old, with friends of the family who canoed and camped in the Boundary Waters and neighboring Quetico Provincial Park in Ontario. Herrick has been coming here ever since, first as a tourist, then as a canoeing and fishing guide. Since 1982 he has owned the Moose Bay Co., a guide service and outfitter. The business, a collection of attractive pine-clad buildings, sits next to Uncle Judas Creek, where it tumbles down a rocky hill and spills into Moose Lake, 20 miles east of Ely.

This springtime fishing appeals to Herrick because it's so visual—and there's so much of it. "The thing that is so enjoyable about smallmouth fishing is that they hit on the surface, they jump, and you can catch numbers," he says. But there are other things to enjoy here as well: the sight of eagles, moose, and ospreys; the bone-chilling howls of wolves and lonesome cry of loons; the endless voices of mighty rivers and light burble of tiny creeks; the firm resistance of a canoe paddle biting the water; the smell of wood smoke and its sting in your eyes; the striking angles of sheer

## FINDING THE RIGHT ROCK

When searching a shoreline for smallmouth, look for rock, but not simply *any* rock. Spawning smallmouth look for a mixture of sand, gravel, and cobble, with cover provided by boulders or downed logs. You should too if you're looking for smallmouth in the spring or early summer.

Shoreline exposed to strong winds and pounding waves are often washed clean of the finer substrate smallmouth need.

On the other hand, back bays are usually filled with muck and lily pads; they may attract bass shortly after ice out, but the bass soon move on, leaving small pike to occupy these areas.

Good springtime smallmouth water usually lies in the transitional areas, neither fully protected or fully exposed to pounding winds. Occasional wave action clears out very fine sediment but leaves coarser gravel and cobble.

cliffs and outcrops cutting the horizontal plane of water. "This is a place where a man can experience more than fishing—perhaps experience things of a spiritual nature," says Herrick.

◄ ◄ ◄

At Herrick's doorstep lies the Boundary Waters Canoe Area Wilderness, a U.S. Forest Service wilderness area stretching more than 100 miles across Minnesota's border with Canada. It encompasses 1.1 million acres with more than 1,400 lakes, ranging from potholes of a few acres to lakes such as Saganaga, Basswood, and Lac La Croix, which spread for miles in every direction and contain dozens of islands. Right across the international border in Ontario lies Quetico Provincial Park, a wilderness area of similar size and character.

To look at these places for the first time on a map is astounding. Lakes, more plentiful than spots on a Dalmatian, are joined by rivulets and portage trails, forming a transportation network used 200 years ago by fur-trading French-Canadian voyageurs and by various Indian tribes before them for hundreds, if not thousands, of years. Because of this abundance of water and its historic use, the area is often called simply "canoe country." And in fact it is: Motorboats are banned in the Quetico and in much of the Boundary Waters. Instead, the thousands of people who fish and camp in these areas set out by canoe.

Herrick introduces newcomers to this country in several ways. He outfits trips with food, camping equipment, and canoes. He provides fishing tips and a short list of places to try. He also provides guided trips into the back country, some of which he leads himself. Whether he is guiding or fishing for pleasure, Herrick will sometimes try for the lake trout that swim in the deepest Boundary Waters lakes, or the walleyes and northern pike that are nearly ubiquitous to the area. But usually, Herrick fishes smallmouth. "That's really the best fishing I have," he says.

This exciting, early-season smallmouth fishing begins shortly after ice out, usually in early May. (Smallmouth can be taken year-round in Canada and the lakes along the border; in Minnesota, they're fair game only after the general fishing opener in mid-May.) During this pre-spawn time, bass are moving into the warmest water possible, even though it may not prove suitable for spawning. Some of the best places to search are mucky black-bottomed bays and the mouths of feeder creeks, which bring warm water from shallow ponds into larger, colder lakes. Also good are "wind-stacked" bays, Herrick says. During warm, sunny weather, a steady wind will blow warm surface water across a lake, "stacking" it in leeward bays. "Something that warms up before the rest of the lake will bring all kinds of fish into it," he says.

In the spring Herrick fishes the shoreline. "We look for the shallowest water we can find," he says. Sometimes he casts fly-rod poppers and divers. Often he uses spinning tackle, peppering the shoreline with medium-sized Rapalas or 1/16-ounce jigs with twister tails. By far his favorite bait, however, is a Tiny Torpedo in natural frog finish. Cast it, let it sit, then work it in small twitches, barely turning the prop on the rear of the plug.

As Herrick works the shallows, he employs his "high-low" method to test deeper water at the same time. As the angler in the bow plugs the shoreline, Herrick, maneuvering the canoe from the stern, drops a jig overboard to bounce along the bottom, from five to 20 feet below. That way, Herrick can catch fish even if they still haven't moved all the way into shallow water or if a cold snap has driven them from shallow water back to the first major drop-off. It's a method he uses in one form or another nearly all season. "You can high-low the rest of your life—spring, summer, fall," he says.

As spawning time approaches, Herrick continues to fish shallow water, using the same plugs and flies, but concentrates on gravel-bottomed bays where bass will actually spawn rather than the black-bottomed bays that were so quick to warm.

## HIGH-LOW FISHING

John Herrick's system of "high-low" fishing derives from a humble and sensible premise: It's impossible to know exactly where you'll find hungry fish. So as one angler casts a surface lure or shallow-running plug toward shallow water, the other paddler drops a jig (either baited or bare) over the gunwale and maneuvers the canoe. Often the fellow paddling will catch more fish than the angler who's fishing full time.

With a little practice, paddlers can switch tactics without changing positions. That is, the person in the bow can dangle a jig while paddling the boat as the person in the stern plugs the shoreline. Taking turns is a good way to maintain boat control even in a stiff breeze.

As water reaches the low 60s, a male bass will herd a female into the shallow nest he scooped out of the sandy, gravelly lake bed and spawning takes place. Contrary to popular understanding, the spawn is not a good time to fish. Not only are there ethical questions about inflicting piscatorial *coitus interruptus*, but the bass are understandably too preoccupied to pay much attention to a lure. Not to worry. If fishing is poor and Herrick suspects fish are spawning, he'll simply move on to another shoreline where, because of deeper water or less sunny exposure, the spawn may not have begun. There he'll find bass eager to gulp down a diver or Tiny Torpedo.

After spawning, females swim away to deeper water, where they are difficult to find and catch. But males stay behind for up to a month to guard the young. They'll pounce on anything that threatens the nest. The fishing can be fast and furious. "We'll have a 50- to 100-fish day," says Herrick, "but they're dinks." He suspects that many of the fish he catches at this time are still too young to spawn but are merely acting out the spawning and nest-guarding behavior. A fisheries biologist I talked to suggested quite a different reason—that with any fishing pressure at all, big males are caught and kept during this period when they are so aggressive, and that only younger, runtier males are left behind.

◄ ◄ ◄

Springtime fishing is easy. What happens next can baffle even those of us who have fished canoe country for years. Often by the Fourth of July smallmouth bass seem simply to disappear.

In fact, says Herrick, most bass *do* disappear, vacating shallow water for deep structure in the main lake basin. If he were fishing an unfamiliar lake, he'd look for long points reaching out from shore and fish the long underwater portion leading to water more than 20 feet deep. He'd also fish points extending from midlake islands. But the very best structure of all, in Herrick's experience, is a "hump," an underwater island, that tops out at between eight and 20 feet deep. The very best have a large flat top about 15 feet deep. "A reef with weeds—that's a great spot."

What are bass doing out here? Probably what most other game fish, including big pike and walleyes, are doing, says Herrick: feeding on tullibees (also called ciscoes), the most prolific and digestible forage in the lake. Pity the poor tullibee: A silvery fish that grows to a foot long, it is the aquatic rabbit—an animal made to be eaten. An immense food pyramid rests on its delectable shoulders.

Tullibees travel in schools. Fall spawners, they move into deeper water as lakes warm in the spring. They suspend over deep water, roaming ceaselessly as they feed on zooplankton—the sorts of microscopic critters spied in a drop of pond water in a junior-high science class. As surface waters warm, they drop into deeper water, hovering in the cool water just above the thermocline—a narrow zone in the middle depths of a lake where the water temperature drops quickly. They will move below the thermocline if there is oxygen there, as is often the case in the large, rocky, infertile basins of canoe country. There's also evidence that tullibees follow plankton in a vertical migration, rising toward the surface early in the day, sinking to their typical deep haunts during midday, and rising once again in the evening.

In the Boundary Waters during the peak of summer, this floating crap game occurs in the open water of the larger lakes. And it is probably for this reason that bass, especially big bass (as well as large trout, pike, and walleyes), flock to humps in the main lake basins—to ambush passing schools of tullibees. "The reefs are barriers more or less," Herrick explains, "places that drive the bait fish closer to the surface or areas that disturb the school's pattern. They have to turn, they get confused and the game fish attack them." When that happens, the water can explode with panicked tullibees and marauding bass.

"It's awesome, incredible," Herrick says. "You'd love it. I have been right in it where there have been hundreds of smallmouth. A cisco is jumping and a smallmouth is in the air right behind it." Herrick makes porpoising movements with his hands and ducks his head as he describes this, as though telling me about the dogfights in Top Gun. "That smallie is on it, in the air, trying to track it. Boom, bam, boom. Ten ciscoes blasting in the air and two or three smallmouth right after them. Just incredible. It's powerful stuff. They've come into our world just briefly, so we've gotten to see some of what's going on down there. I know they're pounding that food like that down below."

Herrick has discovered that bass will rocket upward from more than 15 feet of water to pound a good tullibee imitation. His favorite is the old Zara Spook, a top-water stickbait. (Oddly, the bullfrog pattern with a yellow belly works best, even though the nearest frog may be a quarter mile away.) He casts it out over humps or along weedlines and "walks the dog," twitching the lure so it glides side to side back to the boat. A good substitute for fly rodders is a Dahlberg Diver, retrieved in long strips.

Herrick combines his tullibee trickery with his high-low technique. While the angler in the bow casts a Zara or diver over the hump or along the weedline, Herrick in the stern works a jig (usually tipped with a night crawler or minnow) along the bottom in slightly deeper water.

Sometimes only the deep-water presentation works. In fact, Herrick's largest smallmouth—seven pounds, four ounces—came on a day after a tornado when fishing was generally terrible. They finally found a deep hump where small walleyes were biting, yet something kept grabbing and mangling the cigar-sized fish on the way to the boat. By suspending crawlers a few feet above the bottom, Herrick and his friends began catching huge smallmouth from 30 feet of water. "We caught 30 smallmouth that day over five pounds," he says. "That Mongol Horde out there, cruising pelagically, decided to park."

"How do you find these humps?" I asked Herrick as we fished.

"Just paddling around with my depthfinder on."

But what about those of us who want to travel light? I know I'm loath to make more than one trip to complete a portage. In fact, I view it as a moral failure. Carrying along a portable depthfinder, transducer, and battery seems like a bit too much gear—indeed, a bit too much residue of civilization—for my tastes. So how can I travel light and still manage to catch fish?

First of all, says Herrick, versatile tackle can weigh hardly anything at all. Bring a light- or medium-action spinning rod, a reel with six-pound test line, a spare spool loaded with eight-pound test, and a box of two dozen jigs, ranging from 1/16 to 1/4 ounce, with twister tails. "You can go just with jigs and catch whatever you want," Herrick says. "You can fish them everywhere." If you're willing to carry a bit more, take along a Tiny Torpedo and Zara Spook for surface fishing, a number five Mepps spinner and a couple of steel leaders for pike, a Shad Rap for trolling, and several 1/2- to 5/8-ounce spoons (such as Kastmaster, Little Cleo, or Krocodile) for lake trout.

Many good places can be spotted by sight, Herrick says. Springtime is easiest, when traveling canoeists can cast to good shoreline and the mouths of feeder creeks. Use the high-low system with one paddler casting to shore and the other jigging deep along a breakline. If bass fishing is slow, move into the weedier bays for pike.

Other easy-to-see spots that may hold fish from spring well into the summer are marked by woody cover that litters the bottom in front of beaver lodges and tall fallen trees that bridge the gap from shoreline to deep water. Cast surface lures along the branches and then move close to jig the deep water among the branches and around the tree top.

Currents are also an obvious place to fish—an advantage because they are easy to find; a disadvantage because they get worked over by other anglers. "But for the novice or the person who's traveling—if the weather is stable—currents are great," Herrick says. "You can always catch something." Look for an area where a large stream pours into a lake, and work jigs along the "seam"—the boundary between the downstream current and the swirling eddy currents. Also fish the slack water along shore. Don't overlook areas above a falls or pitch of rapids joining two lakes.

A more subtle current forms in the narrows between two large basins. These currents may be caused by the flow of water through a lake that is part of a large river system such as the Kawishiwi or Basswood, or they may be related to the movement of water pushed against a shoreline by a heavy wind. The current may be subtle, but the combination of moving water and a constriction in the basin often causes fish to gather.

Though deep-water humps are tough to spot without a depthfinder, other deep structure is not so hard to find. A small island, for example, often has a long, tapering point that's visible for much of its length. Simply begin fishing with jigs where the rock disappears into the underwater shadows and work away from the island into deeper water.

The location of an island off the tip of a long point suggests the bodies of land are joined by a saddle of rock that may be deep enough to hold bass. And out beyond the island, more than likely, lies a long, tapering point that leads to deep water. Both these locations are worth fishing. "Plan on fishing several points, not just one," says Herrick. "Expect only one out of three to be good."

Occasionally, as you paddle in or out of a bay, you may notice the tops of cabbage reaching nearly to the surface. Paddle around to learn the dimensions of the weed bed. Fish a Zara Spook over the weed tops and along the edges—especially the deep edges. Try jigs along the deep weed-line, too.

Finally, says Herrick, canoeists can do some effective exploring as they travel. Simply troll a deep-diving Shad Rap parallel to shore as you put on miles. "You can paddle along— just boogie," says Herrick. "Make all the time you want. They run true. They don't roll. They won't mess up your line." Keep the canoe just far enough out that you can't see bottom. If you hook a fish, mark the spot with a landmark on shore. Then go back and fish the area with jigs.

Not only smallmouths, but also pike and walleyes will fall for these techniques—as well as lakers in the deep trout lakes. "You can catch everything," says Herrick. "You can have all the food you want. You can have all the fun you want. You can keep it very simple."

◀ ◀ ◀

I have paddled the Boundary Waters when the aspen leaves are the color of golden apples, the tamarack a smokey amber, the bare birches a brilliant white, the waves a hard, clear sapphire, and the autumn sky the purest blue you've ever seen. The wind blows briskly. Mornings are as crisp as fallen leaves. It is the picture of heaven, except for one thing: There's not a goddamned fish to be found. The shallows are barren. The break-lines and points yield not a single finny critter. It's on just such a mid-September day that Herrick and I set out from Moose Bay Co. Herrick, too, seems discouraged by the autumn cold snap. "Let's go somewhere and fake it," he says as he pulls his jacket collar up around his neck.

Herrick checks his minnow bucket for the last few sucker minnows remaining from a previous trip. "Pretty good minnows for this time of year," he says, and tosses them aboard a wide-beamed johnboat. His canoe lies on a steel rack above the boat like an awning. He uses the johnboat, equipped with a 25-horse, to shuttle paddlers down the brutal fetch of Moose, Newfound, and Sucker lakes to the beginning of the no-motor zone. We jump aboard and fly down the lake, skipping across the waves, against the grain of canoe traffic straining to make progress against the wind. I'm glad I'll be making the return trip under power.

We scoot through the knot of islands plugging the end of Moose Lake, Herrick guiding the skittering boat through a narrow, weaving channel at full tilt.

"You've done this before," I say.

"Oh yeah."

After 20 minutes of flat-out boogie, Herrick runs the boat onto a grass-covered spit separating Sucker and Birch lakes. We tie off the boat, flip off the canoe, and load it up with tackle. "This is a long lake and it runs east and west, so I hope we can avoid most of the wind," Herrick says.

This protected bay lies smooth and inviting. Its limpid shallows, filled with rocks, logs, and rich green shadows, promise countless scores of hungry, gullible smallmouth, pike, and walleyes. Herrick indulges me as I let fly with a monstrous orange and black bucktail I brought for big pike. Canoeists fish the shoreline too much, Herrick observes. I stow the rod and we paddle into the lake.

Herrick's hope to evade the wind is a vain one. Luckily, it pushes us down the lake but promises to be a hassle on the way home. The stern twists and turns as it surfs on the trailing waves. We'll try for pike first, Herrick announces, and at the entrance to a bay begins looking for a deep bed of cabbage he has fished over the years. "If a lake is all rock but has one good weedbed, it will probably be a good spot," he says. "If a lake is all weedy but it has one rock place, that will probably be good." By appearances, Birch Lake's basin is solid granite, so weeds seem like a good idea.

Herrick soon spots the weed tops and moves out beyond what past experience has told him is the outside weedline. I begin flinging the big bucktail shoreward. After just a few casts, it hits something solid. I strike back, expecting to find a big pike. Instead, I winch a three-and-a-half-pound bass to the boat. And it's a largemouth, a scarce character in canoe country. Though completely overwhelmed by the pike-sized rod, it zips and thrashes about the canoe for a minute before I unhook and release it.

Few people fish deep weed beds in canoe country because they are so hard to find, yet they're worth looking for, says Herrick. Sometimes they produce when other spots don't. Once Herrick and several other experienced fishermen had spent all morning pounding rocky humps and shorelines without success. They stopped to eat and to mull over their stunning lack of success when one fellow idly picked up a spinning outfit and cast a big Rapala out over what turned out to be a big submerged weed bed. Retrieving the minnow plug over the weed tops, he hooked and landed a five-pound walleye. With a few more casts, he landed several more walleyes and bass.

Unfortunately, the weeds aren't that generous today. For a half-hour Herrick maneuvers the canoe in the gale, but after the single largemouth, we catch nothing.

"I can paddle," I say.

"No, your job is fishing."

"I'm not doing a very good job of it, am I?"

"Well, it may not be your fault."

Finally, we take refuge on a rocky island to rethink our strategy. Herrick rigs up his portable depthfinder, attaching the transducer with a suction cup to the stern of the canoe. Then we paddle back onto the lake, dodging up a series of back channels to cheat the wind. We emerge next to a long point and follow it into the main lake. Herrick's depthfinder tells him that 26 feet of water suddenly becomes 14 feet as we pass over the hump he is looking for.

He tosses out a marker and we paddle upwind to rig up. We both tie on 1/8-ounce jigs. Herrick uses nothing but bare lead heads with no paint. He reaches into his bait bucket and scoops out a couple of finger-sized sucker minnows, his favorite all-around fall bait for bass, walleyes, and pike. We hook them through the mouth and upward through the snout and drop the jigs overboard, letting out line until they touch bottom. "We used to use a lot of live-bait rigs," Herrick says, "but they were hurting the fish. They were swallowing the hooks." Fish rarely swallow the jig, allowing Herrick to release most of the fish—and all the smallmouth—he catches.

As Herrick occasionally jigs his rod tip to make sure his jig is on or near the bottom, he shows me how to "backtroll" with a canoe. Aligning the stern upwind, he grips the paddle by the throat, with his thumb pointed down toward the blade. He tucks the upper part of the paddle shaft under his arm. Holding the paddle this way, Herrick can scull one-handed as he fishes with the other hand. Thus, he moves the canoe upwind and then lets us drift downwind toward the marker. Then upwind again and slightly sideways to cover new water. Painstakingly, he moves us all around the marker as we bounce jigs and minnow off the bottom.

"Working on this book, I've fished with bait more than I ever have before," I mention.

"That's because you're fishing with guides," says Herrick, who considers bait a big advantage during a fall cold front.

My rod is the first to bend: a 1-1/2-pound walleye. As I pull it to the boat, the intact sucker minnow falls from the walleye's mouth and sinks slowly out of my reach.

"Guide's weight—2-1/2 pounds," Herrick quips. "You know guides invented backtrolling so they could present their bait first."

Next, Herrick's rod doubles over.

"Another walleye?"

"No, this is a smallie." Just then a 1-1/2-pound bass leaps from the water and spits out another of our precious sucker minnows.

Soon, my reel sings as another fish peels off line—a small pike. Another sucker minnow gone.

"How do you work your jig?" I ask.

"Oh, I don't do much with it. I just let it hang there and let it wiggle. I look at this fishing from a canoe as a modified slip-bobber system. The canoe is the float. That's why this is so deadly. First we narrow down the strike zone. Then we hang the bait right in there so it stays in that zone for a long time."

As our supply of sucker minnows dwindles with each fish, we switch to night crawlers. Still we pick up middling-sized smallmouth and walleyes. The fish seem to lie not on top of the hump, but along its edge.

We move on, trying a shallow hump that tops out at nine feet and catch nothing—too shallow apparently for this late in the season. Then we move to a deep point that juts into the main lake. In 22 feet of water, we catch several more smallmouth, including one of nearly three pounds that Herrick lands.

"Nice fish."

"Yeah, I liked it."

As summer turns to fall, Herrick explains, the bass move deeper—sliding down along the humps and bars they occupied during summer or moving to deeper haunts altogether. "The most consistent, the most stable place to fish is the main lake structure," says Herrick. "It will hold fish through the worst of weather. It will give fishermen fish through the worst of conditions."

We fish on into the afternoon, catching bass and walleyes. None are trophies, but considering the hard wind, bright skies and nippy air, I'm impressed. When we are down to our last sucker minnow, we call it quits and turn the canoe homeward.

"What's amazing is that we're close to my house, one portage away from a motor route, and there's no one here at all," Herrick says.

Amazing? At some other time, yes. But now the call of a loon sends chills down my back. Dead gray spruce and cedar angle out from shore over the darkening water. We paddle back into the chilling breeze, into the gray waves, into the teeth of a hard frost.

◗◖ ◗◖ ◗◖

## A WILDERNESS MENAGERIE

The voyageurs of 200 years ago probably never saw smallmouth bass—the fish that in Quebec they called *achigan*, or "ferocious." The reason is that smallmouth are "definitely not native" to canoe country, says Steve Hirsch, DNR fisheries program manager.

Most likely the smallmouth was introduced informally via milk can and canoe from watersheds such as the Mississippi River, where it was native, Hirsch says. Some stocking may have occurred during the turn of the century, when smallmouth transplant programs were popular with fisheries managers throughout the country. Yet it was as recently as the 1930s to the 1960s, says Hirsch, that many canoe country lakes first received this exotic. In fact, some lakes are still showing signs of having new, expanding populations of smallmouth.

Exotic though it may be, the smallmouth bass took to the rocky, clear-water habitat as though bred to it. Now it occupies most of the large lakes in the region, including Lac La Croix, Crooked, Basswood, Basswood River, Knife, Moose, Snowbank, Saganaga, and Sea Gull. Scores of small basins also hold smallmouth.

Because of good habitat and generally light, inefficient fishing pressure (it's tricky business fishing well from a canoe!), the Boundary Waters Canoe Area Wilderness and neighboring Quetico Provincial Park produce some of the best trophy smallmouth fishing the upper Midwest has to offer. A four-pounder is likely, a five-pounder is possible, and a six-pounder, though rare, is hardly out of the question.

Canoe country pike and walleyes also come in trophy size. In fact, the Minnesota records of both species came from the Boundary Waters—a 45-pound, 12-ounce pike from Basswood Lake, and a 17-pound, eight-ounce walleye from the Sea Gull River. Pike, especially, occupy almost every rivulet and pond large enough to sustain fish through the interminable northern winters.

Less common canoe country game fish include largemouth bass, various sunfish, and crappies. Lake trout swim in many of the deepest and coolest lakes in the region.

## Chapter Eleven

><

# THE MYTHICAL MUSKIE:
## *A Very Easy Fish to Catch*

Mark Windels is a casting machine. Standing in the bow, he quickly reels in a bucktail till the leader touches the rod tip, punches the freespool button, thumbs the reel, and launches a cast of 120 feet or more, never moving his left hand from the foregrip. "No lost motion," he says. Then he cranks away on his big ABU Garcia 7000 bait-casting reel as though he's grinding meat. For awhile I try to match him cast for cast, but by midafternoon my back aches as though someone shoved a knife under my right shoulder blade. The tendons in the back of my right hand have stiffened like barbed wire. Yet Windels keeps on casting and grinding at the rate of nearly three casts a minute.

"Is it possible to retrieve these things too fast?" I ask.

"Not really," he answers. If the muskie is the fish of 10,000 casts, Windels aims to get the first 9,999 out of the way as soon as possible.

It's an Indian summer day in early October on a small muskie lake near Hackensack. The sky is blue, the air calm, we long ago peeled off our jackets, and by now it's painfully obvious the muskies in this lake aren't the least bit interested in bucktails. Yet I'm not disappointed. This kind of day, in my experience, is all too common in muskie fishing, and I'm curious to see how an expert like Windels changes his approach in response to this complete lack of success.

Surprisingly, he doesn't. At least, not much. After six hours and not a single strike, Windels sticks to his game plan—motoring from point to point, relentlessly peppering each area with big bucktails. Wouldn't something else work better—jerkbaits or fishing deep with crankbaits?

*Mark Windels: Muskie tournament angler, tackle manufacturer, and champion of the bucktail.*

143

Banish these thoughts, Windels says. They're "negative vibrations." The novice's biggest mistake is constantly changing lures and tactics. "It undermines a good, sound game plan they should stay with," he says.

"Usually it doesn't take any tricks. Usually it's just a matter of catching that fish when he's in a hitting mood. If you base your approach around that, you'll get a fish in the boat a lot quicker than you will by trying to figure out something magical about the lure, the color, the speed of the retrieve.

"We're just biding our time until the fish show up. They're really a very easy fish to catch. They really are. They're extremely predictable. They're very vulnerable. Good fishermen can just clean a lake out. I don't know why all these myths were created."

Muskies—easy to catch? Predictable? This, after all is a fish of imponderable size with an unnerving habit of shadowing a lure to the side of the boat, only to disappear again into the green depths, like treasure dropped overboard and sinking irretrievably toward the bottom.

To Windels the muskie is not a mystery, a fish of legend and indeterminable idiosyncrasies. No, to Windels, a muskie is a toggle switch: It is off or on. And fishing for muskies is not a matter of using a special bait or retrieve, as if seeking magic in a talisman or ritual.

"It's seldom the case of actually trying to fool one," he says. "If we find an actively feeding muskie, he's going to hit this bucktail. He's not going to pass it up for something else. That's true 80, 90 percent of the time."

No, to Windels muskie fishing is a matter of efficiency— efficient boat handling, efficient casting, efficient lures—to make the most of that opportunity when an aggressive muskie and your boat happen within casting distance of one another.

Windels' approach is at once disappointing and reassuring. Disappointing because he strips away the mystique with which the rest of us have enshrouded the muskie. And reassuring because he promises—or comes as close to promising as you can in fishing—that if you simply put in your time with high-percentage methods, you will catch a muskie. It's as simple as that. "I know this worked in the past," he says, referring to the routine we are engaged in today. "I'll just use it till it works again, and it always does."

Windels would know. The long-time muskie tournament angler, tackle manufacturer, and champion of the bucktail has been a "muskie purist," in his words, for 20 years, catching trophy fish at a rate that astounds those of us who think of muskies as the fish of 10,000 casts. In his best year he landed 80; on his best day he boated nine. You can do the arithmetic yourself, but even Windels isn't up to 90,000 casts in a day—even a long one.

144

The popularity of metro-area sail boarding and swimming might slump if word leaked out that 20-pound muskies cruise the swimming beach and lurk beneath the dock of Lake Harriet near downtown Minneapolis. But it's true: Trophy muskies swim in unexpected places because of the Minnesota Department of Natural Resources' muskie program.

In Minnesota muskies are native to only five rivers and about 30 lakes, including Lake of the Woods, Leech, Cass, several lakes in the Boy River drainage, and others near Park Rapids. The fish's range has more than doubled, however, as the DNR has stocked these spectacular game fish in about 50 lakes, including Mille Lacs, White Bear, Forest Lake, Bald Eagle, Minnetonka, and Harriet.

Several of these lakes support brood stock for the state's hatchery program. Those fish are protected by a 48-inch minimum size limit. As a result the lakes produce some real trophies, even though they lie within easy reach of thousands of muskie anglers. A recent 40-inch minimum length limit will help increase the number of trophy muskies statewide.

Despite the success and popularity of the DNR's muskie-stocking program, don't expect that every lake in Minnesota will soon be filled with trophy muskies. The DNR stocks the fish only in lakes that have adequate forage, no chance of winterkill, suitable spawning areas, and a size exceeding about 500 acres. Most importantly, the lake should have relatively few northern pike, the muskie's chief predator and competitor.

The DNR stocks some tiger muskies, the pike-muskie hybrid, in some heavily fished metro lakes where fish managers want a fast-growing trophy fish that is easier to raise in hatcheries than are muskies. Hybrids do occur naturally but are scarce.

So far, says Ron Payer, DNR fisheries operation manager, stocked muskies haven't shown signs of hurting populations of either game fish or forage species. "We don't anticipate an impact from the muskies, though that's an arguable point," he says. To avoid problems, managers frequently assess fish populations and stock relatively few fish. Mille Lacs, for example, receives fewer than 10,000 muskie fingerlings a year.

Windels grew up in St. Cloud, fishing the Mississippi River for small-mouth bass, walleyes, and northern pike. He had heard of the muskies in that stretch of the river but had never caught one. "Then one of the local fellows caught a 35-pounder. He caught it within five miles of where I was fishing. I figured I was just going to do it. I was going to learn how."

He began flinging big spinners into deep eddies, slack backwaters, and log jams in the river and impoundment above town. "A week later I caught my first muskie—31 inches. I was pretty hooked."

He invested in a Garcia 6000 bait-casting reel, an eight-dollar solid fiberglass rod, and a reelfull of braided black 25-pound test line. Within a month he caught a second muskie. "I killed that, too." And a month after that, on three consecutive days, he landed muskies of 18-1/2 pounds, 29-1/2 pounds, and 24 pounds.

"I was really hooked," he says. "But I started to realize, 'Hey, you can't be catching fish and killing them like that. You're screwing up your own fishing."

It was only natural that a young buck tasting his first sweet success in muskie fishing would want to bring home fish as proof and token of his prowess. "But when I heard about a club that gave out patches and awards for catching a nice fish and letting it go, that made a lot of sense, so I joined Muskies Inc."

It was still a young club, and even so rank a beginner as Windels was shocked by the old wives' tales he heard—"stupid stuff like get a new muskie bait and drag it behind a bicycle for an hour to beat all the paint off it because it will work better that way." And a "tip" for fishing the muskies of the Big Fork River: Bait your hook with a live squirrel and float it on a board down to a muskie's lair before yanking it off. "I still don't know how you're supposed to make that squirrel sit on the board," he says. "People were full of these stories, and none of them were catching any fish. They were getting their two or three muskies a year.

"There's a big mystery about catching muskies. I just never found it to be the case," Windels says. Instead he simply worked over places on the river where he had seen muskies, using what he figured were sensible muskie lures, primarily his tried-and-true bucktail, a Mepps Giant Killer. By his second year of muskie fishing, Windels was the local chapter's top fish-getter. "I just found it was mostly putting in a lot of time—long hours waiting for the fish to go."

Yet he wasn't satisfied with the Giant Killer. He weighted it and tinkered with it until he felt he had a lure that carried farther, looked better, fouled less and, as a result, caught more fish with greater efficiency and less down time. Dubbing the new bucktail Windels Muskie Harasser, he assembled the lures in his spare time and sold them through local tackle shops.

At the time Windels was an agricultural entomologist—a bug man—with North American Phillips, who had earned his Ph.D. at the University of Minnesota. With muskie fishing and tackle making competing with business travel for his time, Windels felt pressed to make a decision. "I thought if I'm going to be on the road promoting a business, it may as well be my own, and it may as well be the fishing tackle business." So, about 10 years ago, Windels Tackle Company became a full-time endeavor. When Windels' wife, Carol, also an agricultural researcher, took a new job with the University of Minnesota Northwest Experiment Station, the tackle company followed, moving from the Twin Cities to the prairie and beet fields of Crookston, which, Windels acknowledges, is "about one of the worst places to live in if you love to fish." The nearest decent muskie lake is almost 100 miles away.

These days, Windels spends many days stuck in front of a television, watching CNN as he assembles muskie lures. "Tying up bucktails," he says, "doesn't take *any* thought." When he's not making lures, he travels the Midwest, convincing tackle store owners to carry his products. And when he's not doing that, he's muskie fishing at his cabin on the Canadian side of Lake of the Woods—or bird hunting or bow hunting or elk hunting. "There's just not enough time in October," he says.

Most muskie fishermen carry their muskie plugs hung around the inside of a Styrofoam cooler or in special tackle boxes the size of suitcases. Windels showed up today with only two flat tackle boxes the size of attache cases—two dozen muskie lures, tops. In fact, those two diminutive boxes could carry all the plugs he ever uses for muskies—and for that matter nearly his entire product line, which is tailored to the no-frills, no-nonsense muskie addict.

His biggest seller is the Muskie Harasser, his original bucktail spinner, souped up now in several variations, including double tails, triple tails, single hooks, magnum, and a small-blade version (for kids, without the capacity for enduring endless wrist pain).

Yet he makes other kinds of baits that even he, as a bucktail specialist, uses on various occasions:

• Muskie Hunter, a slant-faced jerkbait that runs deeper than a bucktail and occasionally perks up muskies that are in a neutral mood and lying deep.

• Whaletail, a torpedo-shaped jerkbait that runs shallower than the

Muskie Hunter. "Why'd you call it Whaletail?" I ask.

"I had to think of a name no one had used before," he says.

• Surface Buzzer, a weedless muskie-sized buzzbait Windels uses in slop and other heavy cover.

• Muskie Chugger, a tail-heavy surface plug based on a saltwater bluefish popper, but bigger. He uses it in June, when muskies have finished spawning but still occupy shallow bays. "You can throw it a mile," Windels says. He sits in one place and fan casts much of the bay without moving, to avoid spooking fish.

There's one plug Windels doesn't make that he wishes he did—the Believer, a huge wobbling plug that looks like a plastic manatee. He occasionally trolls one deep along breaklines and deep points when shallow-lying fish show little interest in his baits. "Trouble is, when they're turned off in the shallows, they're just as turned off down deep," he says. Besides, "it's something of a sacrilege to troll and not appreciate the follow—the unique behavior of the muskie."

Yet it's the Harasser that Windels uses perhaps 90 percent of the time. "Bucktails catch most of the muskies caught anywhere," he says, grinding away without a break. "They're the most efficient type of lure for muskies, mainly because they work the shallows better than any other bait. That's where I make my living—up in the shallows. That's where most of the catchable fish are and most of the population. They go where the food is."

◀ ◀ ◀

## CATCHING MUSKIES ON A FIGURE EIGHT

Because of the muskie's unusual habit of following a lure but not striking, you can land a lot more fish by learning a maneuver called the "figure eight." Windels figures he catches as many as a quarter of his fish with this technique, which to my knowledge is used in no other kind of fishing.

"When you get a follow, you're going to want to reel your lure right up to the leader," Windels says. "In one nice continuous motion, you're going to make a great big figure eight, like this," he says, bending at the waist, stretching his arms, and reaching with the rod tip as far past the bow of the boat as possible. With the lure two to three feet underwater, he sweeps the rod tip back toward the stern as far as he can and then to the bow again, tracing a figure eight fully 10 feet tall. "It should be big," he says.

"You want to keep sight of the lure and move it as if you're taking it away from the fish. He won't take it if it looks easy. Just like a cat—if it's too easy for them, they don't want it. So you have to play keep-away.

"Pretty soon he'll look like he actually wants it. You can see an aggressive behavior. Then you just sort of set him up. When you get him to come up right behind it, turn it to the side like the bait is going to make a quick getaway. He'll just open his mouth, go to the side, and grab it. Then you can stick him." To keep from yanking the bait away, feel the weight of the fish before setting the hook.

Windels, who uses 36-pound test braided Dacron line, sets his drag nearly as tight as he can. "You don't want any give," he says. "On very heavy equipment, the fish is going to respond by coming at you, not away from you. He's going to fight it out at the surface. You'll have two to three seconds to back the drag off just a little bit.

"I've broken the line on one fish that did make a power dive—that's one fish out of a couple hundred hooked on figure eights. It's not a problem."

Bucktails are one of the most effective baits to use in a figure eight because they never stop turning—one reason Windels favors them. Jerkbaits and topwaters don't have as much action, and crankbaits often spin out during the maneuver.

Why would a fish too wary to strike on the retrieve suddenly get suckered by a figure eight? Windels suspects the quickly turning lure resembles bait fish trapped against a wall of weeds or other cover. "They get used to that kind of escape pattern," he says. "So it looks very natural to them when they see a bait figure eight."

Interestingly, pike rarely fall for the ruse, Windels says. They flare from the lure as soon as they spot the angler looming overhead.

---

This penchant for shallow water is just one of many characteristics that distinguish the muskie from its outwardly similar relative, the northern pike.

As most anglers know, muskies grow faster and larger. The 69-pound, 15-ounce world record muskie (from the St. Lawrence River in New York

State) outweighs the North American record pike by more than 50 percent and the champion European pike by 27 percent.

Muskies seem more specialized in their habitat needs and are certainly more restricted in their range. While pike range throughout the northern hemisphere from St. Cloud to Siberia, muskies occupy only selected streams and lakes in the eastern United States and southern Canada. In Minnesota, muskies are native to scattered lakes in the Park Rapids area, the big walleye lakes of the upper Mississippi River watershed (such as Leech and Cass), and the lakes of the Boy River system near Hackensack. They also live in a few relatively clear, medium-sized rivers: the Mississippi (above the Twin Cities), St. Croix, Big Fork, Little Fork, and Rainy (which empties into Lake of the Woods, where trophy muskies abound in the Canadian portion).

Two fish that look as much alike as the pike and muskie are bound to compete in waters where they coexist. Both fish, with their fins set far back on their bodies, ambush prey with a short, quick burst of speed. They compete for the same large prey species, such as suckers, perch, and tullibees. This competition may help explain why pike are more widespread than their larger relatives. Pike are more aggressive and less selective than muskies, suggesting that pike would usually win in a race for forage.

European researchers have found that even blind pike can catch bait fish, homing in on prey by vibration alone. Muskies are much more dependent on sight. As a result, pike have an edge over muskies in murky water, such as the algae-ridden water of a marshy prairie lake or the turbid backwaters of the lower Mississippi.

Muskies, however, have better night vision. Pike nearly always stop feeding at sundown, but muskies continue to locate food by the faint light of the moon or stars. In fact, some anglers feel that in clear lakes where fishermen and boaters churn up the water by day, muskies feed mostly by night. The steady putter of a slowly retrieved Musky Jitterbug or snakelike wake of a Hawg Wobbler call in big muskies during hot summer nights, but such inducements are almost a complete waste of time with pike.

Competition between pike and muskies becomes most acute, however, in the weedy bays and backwaters where both species spawn. Muskies arrive in spawning grounds about two weeks to a month later than pike. By the time muskie fry hatch, a horde of ravenous and mobile pike fry are poised to eat them. (Researchers once stocked a pond with 25,000 pike fry and an equal number of muskie fry. The young cannibals set to work. After a month, 400 pike remained. Only four muskies survived.) In lakes and streams with a lot of pike and excellent spawning marshes, muskies apparently don't stand a chance. The two species seem to coexist only where pike numbers are modest, as in some rivers and large windswept lakes. In some lakes, such as Leech and Cass, researchers have discovered that muskies have adapted their spawning habits to avoid newly hatched pike. Muskies in these lakes lay their eggs on bottom vegetation in the deeper areas of spawning bays, well away from the flooded shoreline vegetation where pike spawn.

But the pike-muskie difference of greatest consequence to anglers is the muskie's tolerance for warmer water. Whereas pike, once they reach about seven pounds, seek out spring holes in rivers or cool, well-oxygenated depths where they cruise for pelagic fish such as tullibees, muskies often tuck up in shallow cabbage, bulrushes or timber, as though they were bass with canines.

"Muskies are very content to lay in two feet of water," Windels says, winging a bucktail onto a weedy flat, cranking the moment it hits the water, and retrieving it back to the boat, where the water is 20 feet deep or more. All day we have traveled the perimeter of the lake, stopping wherever a point, usually rimmed with bulrushes, scoots underwater, forming a visible flat for 100 yards or more before dropping off into deep water. Cabbage-covered flats about six feet deep are ideal, he says. "Muskies will come right up and lay on top of that. They like to get minnows or suckers up on top. If they can chase them off the flat out into the open, they can run them down. A little fish looks like it's quick until you get it out into the open water. Then they don't look so quick anymore.

"There's a fish!" Windels announces suddenly, as he plunges his rod tip into the water and begins sweeping the lure in the pattern of a figure eight. But the fish doesn't fall for it. Instead, it flares as it reaches the side of the boat and swims right in front of me as it heads for deeper water. "He was following, but he wasn't very interested," Windels observes.

The habit of muskies to follow a lure to the rod tip, only to disappear without striking, is one of the most maddening aspects of muskie fishing. The best response is a quick figure eight, Windels says (see sidebar on pages 148-149). Beyond that, there's nothing much to do but wait.

"Usually the best thing is to leave him for later," Windels says. Easier said than done, of course. Most of us want to keep casting until the fish strikes or the water freezes over, whichever comes first. "You think you're going to fool that fish, so you spend hours working on one fish. You're basically just wasting your time. Sitting there throwing plugs at him is going to do nothing but drive him down or away. You're much better off taking that hour or two and hitting 10 spots and looking for an active fish."

When you *do* return, he says, try a different kind of bait. "Go from a fast-moving bucktail to maybe a slow-moving jerkbait. Change size and color and speed all at one time. You put all kinds of things in your favor for your next shot."

Even that tack can fail. Windels remembers nicking a huge muskie on a purple Harasser. After a half-hour, Windels came back with a jerkbait. Nothing. A half-hour later, a different jerkbait. Nothing. Then a different bucktail. Nothing. Finally, Windels tried the first Harasser. "I'd put on that damn purple bucktail and throw it in and out that son-of-a-gun would come. He followed nine more times that day. Always on the purple. Never followed another bait. It was as if he recognized that that lure had stung him. He wasn't going to hit it, but he sure as hell was going to chase it every time it came near."

Sometimes you simply have to wait until a change in weather causes fish to begin biting. "Then go back where you saw each of those fish and pick 'em off one at a time." For that reason it's important to note the location of all your follows. Once during a tournament Windels and a partner fished all day with plenty of follows but no strikes. Suddenly, they noticed the fish had begun to perk up. They retraced their steps and boated four fish in a single hour, good for second place.

Yet today, it's not to be. After eight hours of fishing, we've seen only three follows. Given a second chance, none reappear. As it becomes apparent that nothing short of dynamite will rock these muskies from their indifference, even Windels is forced to concede defeat.

As we troll back to the landing, I quickly compute that during the last eight hours, we have each unleashed 1,000 casts or more. But on a day like today, even the magic number—10,000—may not be enough to change a muskie's mind. The switch is off.

◄ ◄ ◄

**Greg Breining** is the managing editor of *Minnesota Conservation Volunteer* and author of several books, most recently *Wild Shore* (Minnesota, 2000), his account of traveling Lake Superior by kayak. His travel articles and essays have been published in *Sports Illustrated*, *Islands*, and *Sierra*, and he is now writing a book about his trip to the mountains of China in search of the nearly extinct South China tiger. More information about his travels and writing is available on his web site at www.gregbreining.com.